"Mama, Why Didn't You Help Me?"

The story of one woman's
fight to reclaim her life
after years of childhood
incest and adult depression

Amber Briéanna Birts

Kristin Hughes
Publishing Corp.
Whitefish Bay, Wisconsin
53217

"Mama, Why Didn't You Help Me?" Copyright ©1990 by Amber Briéanna Birts. All rights reserved. Printed in the United States of America. No part of this book may be used or reproduced in any manner whatsoever without written permission except in the case of brief quotations embodied in critical articles and reviews. For more information, address Kristin Hughes Publications P.O. Box No. 17926 Whitefish Bay, WI 53217

Library of Congress in Publication Data
TXU #452-841

ISBN 0-9630996-0-4

 Kristin Hughes Publishing Corp. 1991

Scripture quotations in the publication are from *The Living Bible* Peoples Parallel Edition
Tyndale House Publishers, Inc. Wheaton Il.
Some names appearing in this publication are pseudonyms chosen to protect the rights of all involved.

ACKNOWLEDGMENTS:

"I would just like to thank a few people who have supported me and made a difference in my life."

Dr. Melvyn M. Wagner of the Wagner Clinic, Milwaukee, WI. Thank you for your patience. I know things got kind of rough there, for a while but we got through it. (I never told you this before Melvyn, but that plant in the window — get rid of it, there's no hope for it.)

To my wonderful **Editor, Kathleen Dale, Lecturer, Dept. of Learning Skills and Educational Opportunity at the University of Wisconsin – Milwaukee**. Thank you is not enough. I think you are terrific!! The time we spent together sharing will never be forgotten. You took what I thought was "nothing" and held it with so much respect and high acclamation. I will never be able to let you know what this did for me.

To Carlos and Norma Felix, my parents. Although you didn't actually birth me out, you saved my life and gave me a place to call home. Papi, I thought we'd get to see forever . . . . I'll miss you. Bendicion.

Special thanks to Marge Osuskz. To Katherine A. Page, my beautiful sister-friend. Thank you for the "bungee cord," the picnic lunches at the beach and for rescuing me from the abyss. "Kat, this one's for you."

Last but never least, thanks to God for giving me the strength to hold on long enough to share my story with all of you.

DEDICATION

Fred, this book is dedicated to you. You have never experienced the pain and trauma of child abuse yet you went through it with me like a champ! You have been there for me every step of the way telling me to hang on, and telling me how important I am to both you and the kids. You knew that I never really wanted to die — I just needed the pain to stop. You have done above and beyond your call of duty. Honey, you held us all together by the quality of life that you have given us.

Thanks for the encouraging talks that we had during the wee hours of the night, and I also thank you for all of the comedy tapes that you made me watch. Most of all I thank you for loving me and not leaving me throughout my periods of deep depression and "neurotic episodes." Without you, I would not be here today, yet fighting for my life. You are my husband, my lover, and "Very-best-most-special-friend-in-the-whole-wide-world."

To Kris and Freddy, I say, thank you. Thank you for putting up with my constant hospitalizations and those awful frozen pizzas! You guys are the best children that any mother could ever hope to have. I love you because you have tried to understand on your own levels, what I went through as an abused child and you have continued to support me by telling me that I am the best Mom in the world!

With love, kisses and
"home-made" fried chicken,
Mom.

In Memory of

Carlos Felix, Sr.
1928-1991

PRELUDE

Mama never told me of "honey-dipped" dreams. She never told me of "cotton-candy" wishes or "strawberry milk" flavored things. Mama never told me that there would be pain, sorrow and misery in my young life. She never told me about child abuse, incest or any of those "terrible" things. She didn't have to — they just were.

"Mama, you never told me nothing!" You just let life happen to me while I experienced it all. Every bit of it . . . broken dreams, broken toys, broken hearts and broken bones. Mama, you never even told me.

"Have you ever seen a scared chicken run, Mama?" Well, that's what your children were, a bunch of "scared chickens" running around "Daddy," afraid to death of having their heads chopped off. Where were you, Mama? Where were you during the times that your beautiful brown children were being led to the slaughter? Their frail little bodies plucked, mutilated, violated and intimidated.

Daddy hurt me, Mama. He tore though my tiny body with his erect penis, and I died a little bit more each time. His dirty body that you wouldn't let near you lay hovering over me like a musty old coat, suffocating me.

I knew that if I could just hold on until he was finished, that I would be okay. If I could just hold out until that all too familiar jerking and that last thrust was over, then I knew that I had made it through yet another session . . . at least until the next time.

Daddy did that to me, Mama, but you didn't know because you weren't there. My only question to you after almost thirty years is, "Where were you and why didn't you help me?"

chapter one

Scrawny and frail, a child with enormous eyes filled with seas of turmoil. Her dark curls fall limply around her slender face. The hand-me-down pinafore dress starched heavily seems to add years to her actual age.

Outside, the wind is howling furiously and the scratching movements of the tree branches against the roof of the closet soothe the dull ache in Brié's chest. The only safe place that she knows is this closet. The walls reach out to embrace her hot face and cool the sting of her flowing tears.

The four walls, the soft velvety wooden floor, old battered toys and hand-me-down clothes, these are her treasures. "Sallyanne" and "Patches" are her friends. It doesn't bother them that Brié is not very pretty, or that her hair is unmanageable.

"Sallyanne" is feeling much better after having recently received a brand new head of hair, candy-apple red yarn sewn ever so gently into her scalp. Brié had chosen the name "Sallyanne" because she didn't want to be called "Raggedy Ann;" it hurt too much.

It wasn't her fault that the apron of her dress didn't match her pantaloons, or that her candy-cane-striped legs had become overly worn with the passing of the years. "Patches" is a wonderful, soft Teddy Bear with lint balls attached to his pot belly. The fact that Patches is missing an arm makes Brié feel especially close to him. She feels that she and Patches have a common bond — they are both tattered, torn and tossed aside.

The distant muffled sounds of screaming voices and dishes breaking penetrate the walls of Brié's hiding place, but she continues on with her tea party. The table had been set by Sallyanne, and Patches waits in anticipation for the double-decker chocolate fudge brownies to slide out of the "Easy-bake Oven."

Brié's beautiful safe place is alive with singing and dancing children in beautiful clothing and freshly polished shoes. The voices are louder now; roaring fills the living room below Brié. She sings louder; her chest pounds harder, harder. Perspiration flows down the little girl's arms and she closes her eyes tightly, fighting both sound and reality.

The door of the closet is snatched open. The music stops. Silence. There he stands, leather strap in hand. The party is over.

Incest is as old as the "Original Sin." This topic has been talked about, over worked, and has somehow managed to put the entire free world to sleep. Incest is one of those "taboo" subjects which everyone agrees is going on, but no one really wants to talk about. It's kind of like cancer — it's a terrible thing but God forbid that "I" should have to deal with it.

I take this stand merely because I have been one of the guilty ones who actually took an active part in the ritual of "hearing no evil" when it came to this subject. Like many people I felt that somehow if we didn't talk about or acknowledge it, "it" would just go away. After all, what is it that these people want? Could it be that they have taken the role of incest victims only to make life miserable for the rest of us? Does the American public have to endure yet another "talk show host" beating the old dog of incest?

Where should we begin to draw the line? When

will these "victims" begin to suffer in silence, allowing the rest of the "normal" world to enjoy the sanctity of peace and quiet?! I can't speak for the entire American public, but when I come home from a long day at the office I certainly don't want to flick on my television set only to find "Oprah," "Phil" or "Geraldo" discussing the horrors of incest!

On May 4th, 1988, a young woman, age twenty-eight, walked into her doctor's office extremely depressed and with thoughts of suicide. She had obtained a successful career in banking and communications, yet for some reason unknown to her she had lost all hope for her life and had only thoughts of doom and depression. Her life had come to a screeching halt and she had been reduced to the level of a "neurotic woman," or at least that's how she was feeling. She was now being told by her family physician that she should seek out a "shrink" for professional help.

The ride up on the elevator seemed to be taking forever. All the unnecessary stops between floors was irritating to Briéanna. "Never in a million years did I think I'd be seeing a shrink! Sick people with mental disorders or people having breakdowns go to see shrinks. I'm not crazy, maybe a little tired and depressed, but certainly not crazy!"

No matter how I tried to rationalize it in my mind, the bottom line was that I was indeed going to see a psychologist. For some reason life was beating the hell out of me and I needed someone to help me to get my thoughts straight.

The psychologist, Dr. Michael Warner, was a tall, handsome man with curly blond hair and beautiful baby blue eyes. "Is this all I get?" I thought. "No Freud? No old man with a bald head? No beard? Where was that traditional tweed suit that I thought all shrinks wore?"

The office was beautifully decorated and smelled of mahogany wood and men's cologne. The book shelves were loaded with books about neurotic women, anxiety attacks, and a bunch of other topics that a "sick-o" like myself should know about. The swivel chair, the plants, the art effects, even the scent of the doctor's cologne seemed to be beckoning me to relax and to spill my guts!

The good doctor, clad in his designer suit, expensive shoes, and a Gucci watch, sat arrogantly across from me with his legs crossed. For some reason I can remember feeling very uncomfortable just sitting there. "Okay already," I thought to myself. "Shrink me, tell me what's wrong with me — anything! But just fix me."

Finally, the great "Demi-God" almighty spoke. "Tell me a little bit about why you are here." All I could think about also was "Why am I here?"

"I don't know," I finally said quietly, trying not to let my voice crack or to show that in any way I was fighting back my tears. "I haven't been feeling very good about myself." There, I had said it. It wasn't as hard as I thought it would be. Maybe now

I would stop sweating. I was trying very hard not to squirm or wring my hands, but this therapy stuff was really a hard thing for me to get through.

"Could you elaborate on that a little bit more, Briéanna?"

"Great," I thought, just what I need: a stupid jerk-of-a-shrink, who can't understand or relate to a simple phrase like "I feel like crap!" Maybe I was in the wrong office. Actually, the guy looked like he couldn't have been more than thirty years old. What could he possibly know about me, psychology, or anything!? "Lately," I finally replied, "I've been really tired and all I want to do is to sleep. From the time that I get up in the morning until it's bedtime again, the only thing that I think about is sleep."

A very uncomfortable silence fell over the room as I waited for him to reply, but guess what — he didn't. He stared at me and I quickly looked at the floor. If there had every been a time in my life that I truly wanted to crawl under a rock, this certainly was it! "I can't believe that I'm gonna pay this guy eighty bucks!! And for what?" I fumed to myself.

The digital clock was turning minute by minute and all I could do was to play with my fingers and try not to cry, but it wasn't working very well, because the tears were flowing down regardless. Of course, the only visible box of Kleenex in the room was located miles away from my reach, or so it seemed. As much as I both wanted and needed that kleenex I sat frozen. In my mind, that tissue stood as a barrier between the doctor and me. (As you can see, I was in need of some serious therapy.)

"Well," I thought, "I could tell him a little about myself or my marriage, or how I hate sex."

"Yeah, right; Get real Brié." I felt this way because I could not imagine exposing such personal aspects of my life to someone that I had just recently met. That kind of stuff I barely wanted to talk about with my own husband Fred, not to mention talking about it with a perfect stranger.

"What are you thinking?" Dr. Warner finally asked.

"Oh, nothing." Slowly I looked him dead in his big baby blues. "Do you get many patients, like me, who just come here and sit?" I asked, trying to break the silence.

"Yes. I realize that this is a new experience for you and it's hard to come into a strange place and communicate your feelings to a strange doctor, but I assure you that everything that you say to me will be held in the strictest of confidence and respect." I smiled shyly at him and failed to reply.

After his wonderful speech on "confidentiality," I felt a little bit more at ease, and we made idle "chit-chat" until he finally uncrossed his legs and stated that my time was "up" and that we should do this again next week. "How's 1:45 next Wednesday?"

"That's fine, thank you." What a rip-off I thought, as I rose to leave.

"Briéanna, will you please leave the door open behind you?" That's a first, I thought sarcastically. In the movies the shrinks usually say something like, "Will you please close the door as you leave?" But I guess this wasn't the movies, was it? Nope, this was life — the real thing!

Outside, the wind was cold and sharp. All the earth seemed to be standing still. Depression is a strange thing. I sometimes find it hard to put into words all the feelings of sadness that come from nowhere. I don't think anyone really wants to die when they are being consumed by the pain of depression. Suicide seems to be a temporary answer for a long-term problem that one just can't face. As for myself, I just wanted the pain to go away so that I could breathe. Yes, there are still days that I wrestle with thoughts of suicide and giving up. Those days seem to go on forever when I am experiencing them. The days turn into nights and nights into daylight again and it seems to be never-ending. My only hope for what most people would call a "normal" life was now a preppie, Jewish shrink and a gnawing will to survive that came from only God knows where.

chapter two

I was conceived. I was born. That's just about it. From what I hear, there was nothing else that was special about that day. That's the story of my life. I never felt that I was special, or that I really mattered much to anybody. I was just another child born into an already overly-expanded family of violence. I was the second youngest born out of six. My family, I learned at an early age, thrived on abuse. Verbal, physical and yes, sexual abuse. My mother was abused by my father and somehow through all of her abusive situations she allowed this cycle to seep down upon her children.

When I was a little girl I would read books about the "Mama Bears," or the eagle and her young and it seemed that they spent their whole lives and energy feeding and protecting their young babies. Even in the animal kingdom there seemed to be some sort of "protection instinct" that most mothers had in common — but not at our house. We weren't animals were we? It hurts, but I will always remember my mother as unprotecting when it came to her children and the traumatic abuse that we had to endure on an on-going basis.

I was given the name Juanita Faye Collins at birth, and wore that name like a dirty old rag for most of my life. Most people didn't understand the great urgency that I felt to change my name when this whole business of the incest came out. I was constantly having flashbacks of my father screaming out my name. He said it with such filth and violence, that the very thought of it would make me quiver, and I began to hate my own name. I would awaken from a cold sweat with nothing but fear and the remembrance of his loud voice screaming out my name. "Juaniiiita!!!" It was enough to make a "Rose," as beautiful as it is, want to be called a "Lily."

I wasn't in denial of the whole turn of events, but I think Shakespeare said it best when he said, "A rose by any other name would smell as sweet," meaning I was still the same person. This was a hard thing to get across to people. It wasn't until I had been married for eleven years, however, and the mother of two children, that I conjured up enough of this nerve to tear off that rag-of-a-name and clothe myself with a name which I felt suited me. I chose Amber. Amber Briéanna Birts. I don't know how or why but with all of the things going on and the different emotions that I was feeling, I thought I felt like "Amber." The "Briéanna" part came from speaking a little French, and I also liked the thought of coming up with a name of my own, sort of like a gift to myself, a name that was different.

Memories of the first house in which we lived are scary ones. The house reeked of dead mice and the smell of cigarettes. At night I would pretend that my family lived in a palace and the dead mice, which lay in the traps set by my mother, were merely wild life caught for me by my prince. I wish that I could say my imagination made them disappear but it didn't. With every "snap" that rang out in the night, I knew the fact of the matter was that another mouse had been caught by its tail and was lying somewhere in the house dead, waiting to be flushed down the toilet.

The house was dark and damp. I shared a room with my younger brother, while my three older sisters shared the other bedrooms. I hated sharing a room with him. I know now after a few years of intense therapy that even back then, at that tender age of five, my uncomfortableness regarding my little brother stemmed from my acute awareness of my own sexuality. I hated my little brother. Why did he have to be a boy? Why did he have to have a penis like daddy? I didn't want him near me. There were times that I purposely hit him or was mean to him because of his penis. Just the knowledge that he possessed this weapon scared me. Being aware of these kinds of sexual things seemed common to me; my father saw to that. If there was one thing that I knew about at that age it was sex and violence. I sometimes got the two of them mixed up.

After all, how was I supposed to know that when my father called softly for me to come into his bedroom to have sex with him, that that very act in itself was violence? It didn't feel that way to me at the time. I didn't want it to feel that way. After all, I was his daughter, and he was my father. I wanted him to love me, to hold me and to protect me. I prayed for it and pretended that the coarseness of his fingers digging into my vagina and rectum were just that — touches of love. When he demanded that I insert his penis into my mouth and suck it "real hard," I did. I always did just like Daddy ordered, just like a "big girl." Then I waited for that violent eruption of white "goop" which always followed.

"Did I do it right, Daddy?" I would always ask him as I fought hard to ignore the stench of his semen coming up from my throat and fighting back the urge to vomit.

"Just shut up," he answered. "I'll tell you when you do something wrong."

I would lie stiffly next to this man afterwards trying very hard not to move an inch. I would inhale his thick cigarette smoke and wait to be dismissed. I would wait to see if there was anything else that I could do for Daddy. I wanted to please him. That was so important to me. To be a "big girl" and to please Daddy with our little secret. A secret which would later cause me to try and commit suicide, to endure years of psychiatric hospitalizations and to later be declared mentally disabled by the state of Wisconsin.

That's what my daddy did to me. My mother was nowhere, nowhere around. Even if she had been there, I wonder to this day what she could have actually done. We all knew that she was powerless and had no control over our father. Sometimes at night we would listen to him beating her. The furniture would crash, dishes would break, and Mama would be begging him to stop hurting her.

We each knew what it felt like to be beat by Daddy. On those nights, it seemed that her crying would go on forever and as much as we wanted to help her, we couldn't. We lay helplessly listening to her tiny little voice crying and pleading, begging a man whom she had married years and years ago to stop hurting her. "I'll never get married," I said to Patches my Teddy Bear, "Never."

I wiped the tears from my eyes and retreated into my world of pretense, where everything was good and clean and safe, my special quiet place where little girls didn't have to have secrets with their daddies. It was marvelous and magical and there would always be lovely music playing and lots of good things to eat. But most of all there would be no men with penises and there would be no mice.

One night, Mama needed bread from the grocery store, so she went out grocery shopping and didn't return until extremely late. My sisters Jerry and Ann went along with her to help out. The smaller children were left alone with my sister Terry. We played house and tried to occupy the long stretch of time that seemed to be going by. Terry tried not to show it but I know that she was beginning to get scared though no one said anything. We sat huddled in the middle of the living room floor just waiting. Every time we would hear a voice or a car pass by, one of us would peek out of the front window to see if it was Mama. Finally, there was a crash at the front door, and there seemed to be fighting or wrestling going on. Suddenly there it was — the all-too-familiar sound of Mama crying and screaming. We knew then that they were home, and that

Daddy was with them — drunk. My sister Ann came through the door crying and helping my sister Jerry to lug my mother through the door.

We all just stood there frozen, too afraid to even ask what had happened. My eyes were paralyzed by the blood on her coat and face, and the gun that my father was waving in his hand. Fear overtook that small little alley household and every child that my mother had began to cry and scream. All we saw was a drunken and staggering man waving a pistol and hurling obscenities at everyone. "Mama, Mama, what happened?" my little brother asked, scared to death.

"Shut-up and mind your own business," my father replied.

The scarf which she was wearing was saturated with blood and she had a large bruise on one side of her face. After the noise had died down, and Daddy had gone back out drinking, my sisters told us about how Mama and Daddy were arguing in the car over how he had left them stranded for hours at the grocery store and how Daddy pulled out his gun and began to beat Mama with it and dragged her by her hair out of the store. This went on until the police were called. Mama said she didn't want to press any charges: she told the police that everything was alright.

I hated Mama.

For as long as I can remember I have always feared my father. He was a short man with a deep voice and a very short temper. His idea of running a home was to run it in the style of the military. Mama called him "shell-shocked" but anyway, we could only talk when spoken to, answer only with

"Yes Sir" and "No Sir" and we were always to be at his beck and call. There was no room for compromise. The repercussion for being found guilty for any breach of conduct was to be severely beaten. The beatings came unprovoked and without warning. There were beatings for not cleaning up our rooms, there were beatings for forgetting to wash the dishes and then there were the beatings that came from just being a child.

I can't remember the exact day or time when my father started sexually abusing me. I only know that I was deathly afraid of him. When he walked into the room I froze. The earliest memories that I have are of the age of four. Not only did he abuse me, but he also allowed his friends to abuse me. It was like some kind of a joke with him. There is one man in particular, who was a friend of the family. One of his drinking buddies. We called him "Uncle J.D." Sometimes Daddy would play cards with him and lose. I guess Daddy struck up some sort of deal with this man to pay off his gambling debt, and I was a part of the deal. "Now, I want you to look real pretty for Uncle J.D. and do whatever he says," my father said to me.

I can remember my father trying to dress me up to look real pretty for this man. He put me in a frilly dress and slapped some vaseline on my face. "Don't be acting like no baby. You know what to do and you better not be crying, like he's hurting you, do you hear me?"

"Yes Sir," I mumbled, not quite sure of what was going on.

Uncle J.D. was as tall as the sky and had a bald head, with a dark brown mole on one side of his face. He took me upstairs to my bedroom and laid me on the bed.

He spoke softly and told me that we were going to play a little game. Well, when he started to pull down my panties I knew the game. And I could play it well. I played it without feelings and I didn't even cry. Better yet, when the "game" would be over I knew how to keep it a secret. He didn't talk rough like Daddy. He was nice. He asked me if it hurt. "No, it don't hurt; it feels real good." (That's what Daddy told me to say.)

The bed made a very loud thumping noise as he penetrated my body with his penis. He was bigger than Daddy, but it didn't hurt like when Daddy did it. He used his tongue a lot to lick my vagina, and stopped from time to time to ask me if I was sure that I was okay . . . but I was somewhere off in another land . . . escaping.

I could feel the sun shining brightly through the window and I stared out into space blocking out as much as I could. I don't know why, but I felt dirty. Dirty and nasty and I wanted to disappear, but I couldn't — because I was a good girl and good girls don't make trouble for their daddies. They do just what he tells them to do.

On the days when my mother went to work as a housekeeper, I was left alone with Daddy. I guess this was a perfect time for most of the abuse to happen, because during therapy with Dr. Warner, these were the times that I recalled first, regarding the abuse. My mother was working and my sisters, who were quite a bit older than I was, were in school. My little brother, Ben, was always somewhere hiding so as not to get in the way of Daddy.

We all found that the best way to get through life with him was to make yourself as invisible as possible. I guess that's what Ben did during those times. When asked to this day where he was and what he was doing, he has no recollection.

When Daddy would summon me into his bedroom, the room would be dark, and would reek of cigarette smoke and filthy sheets. Sometimes he would just lie there with his boxer shorts on and point to his penis and I would begin to masturbate him. (I knew the routine.) Other times, he would already be naked and would pull back the sheets to expose himself to me and motion for me to climb into bed with him. Those were the worst times. I didn't know what to expect. My head would swim with fear as he touched my body. His penis was extremely frightening to me because sometimes he would just lie there and laugh as it did this little "dance" all by itself. He would make me watch as he used his muscles to manipulate his organ. I knew if I showed fear it would only be worse for me, so I pretended. I was good at it, so I pretended. . . . I was someplace else, anyplace but his bedroom. . . . I was a princess and lived in a beautiful castle with wonderful horses and everything was gorgeous.

This was the only time when he wasn't hitting me. His touching me was okay, I told myself, because he would tell me that I was pretty and sometimes he said that I was his favorite girl, and that he would always be there, whenever I wanted him. He said if Mama ever found out about us that she wouldn't like it. He said that we couldn't tell anyone because they wouldn't understand about our special relationship.

I wished I could understand about our relationship. Sometimes he acted as if he loved me and touched me softly, and other times he beat me and tore through my body with anger and rage. This always left me confused and it also made me cry. I cried because I was trying to be good, and yet it was never enough for Daddy.

When it was all over I pretended not to hurt. I would just wipe the blood away and hide in my closet. I spent a lot of time in my closet. It was a place where I could be alone and there was no Daddy. There was no one to hurt me and there was no one to touch my body. In my closet there was only me. Just me and the four walls, and the cold. It was in my closet that I learned most of my survival skills in regard to the incest. I became a cold and distant child with no emotions. At school I made no friends and talked very little. My thoughts revolved around myself, my pain, and my deep dark secret.

There was no one to help. No one to tell and no one to care. What had I done in all of my short life to deserve such pain? I carried the pain around like dead weight, secretly praying and hoping that help would appear from out of nowhere to save and rescue me. Today, I'm almost thirty years old and I'm still waiting for that magical person to step in and help me. I feel that I need someone other than myself who is strong and protecting to help me carry the weight of my incest. I need someone to help me carry this burden . . . just for a minute. . . .

chapter three

Therapy. I hate therapy. But it was a place to go. A place to try and sort out my thoughts. "Let me see," I thought to myself, "I walk into this doctor's office and talk to him about my feelings, he says nothing and then I pay him eighty bucks? Boy what a deal!" At times, Michael really got on my nerves with his smugness. I wished that I could be that smug. Also there was the matter of the "Kleenex box" which he had in his office. A box of Kleenex in a handmade, knitted covering — you know, the ones that looked like your grandma made? Well, anyway, the stupid thing was always empty! I don't know about you, but to me, this was some kind of psychology at work, saying "Now, Brié, there will be none of that crying crap in this office, so just knock it off." I would actually reach for the tissue box and there would not even be one single solitary tissue in there! How is a person supposed to let go and allow herself to be cleansed of any kind of pain or grief when she can't even have a decent cry?

Besides the tissue thing, Michael (Dr. Warner) was okay. We agreed that I would call him Michael because of my hang-up regarding my being in therapy. Calling him Michael sort of made it seem as though I was talking to a good friend instead of someone who had spent his life studying psychology.

It made him seem more real — like a friend, and that's exactly what I needed, a friend to talk to. Someone that would support me and tell me that I wasn't crazy and that I was okay. Michael would tell me time and time again that he would never stand in judgment of me or my past. I really wanted to believe him. I wanted to trust him but I guess I never really did.

"Trust" wasn't something that I was very comfortable with — I didn't truly know or understand it. I had a real fear of being exposed and rejected. I didn't want to allow anyone close enough to me to hurt me. Besides, I felt that if he truly knew everything about me and my past, even he would somehow reject me. (Michael says that my thinking is indicative of my upbringing and has to be eliminated in order for me to ever get the help that I need.) "What the hell does he know!"

Many times in therapy, I really wanted to let go and tell it all. I wanted to scream and yell and cry and fall on the floor. I could imagine myself lying there on the floor, beating it like it was my father's head, kicking at the carpet and just having a total "fit." However, I never did. I kept it all tight and neat and clean. I had a way of intellectualizing over what had happened to me. I would arrive at Michael's office in my nice little "Nancy Reagan" apparel, sit down politely, cross my legs and act as if we were there to discuss the "state of the union." I tried to stay as distant as possible.

Most of my adult life has been spent starting and stopping various projects. I have worked as a beautician, a banker, an escrow analyst, a sales representative, dental assistant, police telecommunicator and a marketing representative for the Milwaukee Symphony Orchestra! In each of these fields I have been promoted and told of my "wonderful" qualities and abilities. Once, while working in the banking field, I entered a speech contest held on the local level by the Savings and Loan Industry, and I won first place. Winning the local competition allowed me to compete on the state level, where representatives from all over the state of Wisconsin competed. The object of the contest was to both write and deliver a speech regarding the Savings and Loan Industry. Each contestant was judged strictly on the content of that speech entered, and its delivery.

I recall being seated at a table with other contenders, wishing everyone else good luck, not even aware of the fact that my name had just been called as the winner. It was an experience that I will never forget. For once in my adult life I had been good enough. I had won first place in this state competition. The excitement of the whole thing was wonderful, yet I felt that it wasn't really happening to me. It wasn't real. It was all one of my unbelievable dreams and I would soon wake up and find it all gone. That's how I have treated most of the successes in my life. I never allowed them to seem real to me, or to have any positive impact on me because beneath it all, I am yet fighting hard with my problem of low self esteem. I am trying to work it all out in therapy, but this is something that I have lived with all of my life. I constantly live with feelings of being a Whore and not being of any worth.

Psychotherapy has a "wonderful" way of bringing all that stupid crap that one has hidden beneath the surface to life, and believe me there was a lot of crap in my life that needed to be brought forth. The painful memories of my childhood, which I had repressed, begin to bubble up and spill out like a pot coming to its boil, and I hated it. It left me weak. It left me feeling exposed and it left me feeling dirty. Afterwards, when I would return home from a stressful session with Michael, I would always have a horrible night. I would wake up wet with perspiration and terror, wondering if any of this stuff could have really happened! It was a form of denial that I would go into in order to buffer the pain of it all.

While wide awake, in a deep depression, one day I had a flashback. The room was dark and smelled of cigarettes and sweat. "Hand me my cigarettes." My father's voice sliced through the silence like a knife. I was about ten years old, and was lying in bed next to my father with my panties around my ankles. In this flashback, I remember reaching for that shiny red pack of "Winstons" and his cigarette lighter.

I watched him as he inhaled the cigarette slowly and then deliberately blew the smoke into my face. Quickly I snatched my thoughts back to the present. "It just can't be," I said over and over again. I thought if I said it long and hard enough that it would go away. But it didn't. "What was I doing lying naked in bed with my father?" Did I really want to know? It wasn't a dream because I wasn't asleep. The terror of it all brought tears to my eyes and I felt as though I had opened a "Pandora's Box." Nevertheless, I wanted to know. I had to know the truth of that day, regardless of how painful. So I lay back on my pillow and allowed the horrible memories of my incestuous relationship with my father to flow. What I saw, felt and remembered was not pretty.

I don't remember the day, hour, or sequence of things, but I know that the incest had been going on for a long time. For years. In the particular scene that I was remembering, the shades of the bedroom window were pulled shut and there was a hint of sunlight creeping through the cracks of the worn out shades. Mama wasn't home, and I don't know where anyone else was. The only thing that I was cognizant of was the stinging between my legs and the numbness of my rectum. I was a little girl with a tiny body that felt old, used and tired.

My father laughed as he pushed my head down between his legs and demanded that I perform oral sex on him. The floor was made of smooth dark wood and the bones of my knees hurt as I went about this act. This scene is so vividly impregnated within my mind because I had always been petrified of mice. I can remember wanting my father to hurry up and ejaculate. I was more afraid of the mice that might be running around than I was of the disgusting act that I was performing on him. I kept wondering what I was doing wrong. After being down on my knees for what seemed like forever, I started to cry.

I didn't understand the roughness of his manner as he began to slap me. I guess the fear of the mice had made such an impact upon me that it caused me to bear down too hard on his penis with my teeth. I can still remember the sting of the slap. At that time "reality" and not one of my stupid fantasies over came me. All of my secret hiding places eluded me. I was finally feeling the true impact of our "secret," and it was something that I no longer wanted to bear alone. I wanted to tell, but of course I couldn't because in my mind I was a slut and a whore and I didn't deserve any kind of asylum. These negative "tapes" of my father calling me a whore yet haunt me. I try to deal with these feelings in therapy, but it's always the same: "It wasn't your fault, you were a child. . . ." Sometimes, to be honest, I just wanted to slap the life out of Michael when he would start that crap! It wasn't helping me.

I felt that I could only divulge bits and pieces of how I was really feeling to Michael. Even though he was my therapist, there was an element of shame that I felt. I once heard that the spoken word is so powerful, that once it's out there no amount of wishing is going to allow you to take it back. Sometimes during our sessions, I felt like the lowest cretin alive and just wanted to slither like a snake right out of the door and into the nearest sewer.

I know this may be hard for some readers to understand, but when the monster of incest is banging on your front door it's hard to think rationally. As hard as I fought, there were still times when I allowed myself to be sucked in by my own self-pity and depression. It enraged me, because it seemed that my reflective thinking, positive affirmations, and even my going to therapy to talk about this junk was rendering me unfunctional!

"My God," I wondered, "How can talking about something which has caused so much pain be healthy?" I didn't feel as if I were making progress or having any dynamic breakthroughs. I felt like I was on the verge of a mental breakdown! Therapy almost felt like a lair of masochism — a place to go to see just what "straw" it was going to take to break that proverbial "camel's back," and send me running and screaming off to the nearest mental health facility.

During therapy, Michael dealt with me in a soothing manner, but most of the time I sat paralyzed. I was numb. The sudden twist on my life was unbearable. When I didn't want to talk, or when the pain was too hard to bear, I would just sit for the majority of our session and look at the floor, holding onto my tissue, fading back and forth in my mind, as to why I was there.

"What are you thinking?" His voice seemed to come from nowhere.

"I don't think I can take any more of the flashbacks that I've been having," I stated quietly. "Every time I think that they are over, here comes another one. It's just too much, and I can't take it anymore."

"I know it seems like a lot to handle, but you'll find that it gets easier if you talk about it."

"Yeah, right," I thought. "I eat, sleep and drink incest, and he wants me to talk about it?" I wanted it to stop. I wanted to get on with whatever was left of my life. Furthermore, I hated him!! Just the fact that I had to pay someone to listen to the filthy details of my shattered life was enough to make me want to jump off of the nearest bridge.

As I rode the elevator down to the first floor, I felt as if I were in a trance. People walked by, but they didn't really exist. Some smiled at me, but I didn't exist. The only thing that I could feel was my pain, my tears, my incest.

My car seemed to be parked a hundred miles away as I tried to make my way to it. I drove home in a daze. At times, I found myself fighting off the urge to steer my car right into a tree. "If I can just make it to my bed, then I'll be all right." That's where I spent most of my waking hours lately, in bed. In bed and with Dr. Warner in therapy. Nothing helped. Nothing made the pain go away, nothing.

After days of this disposition, and my inability to get out of bed, I agreed to check into the local hospital for depression. That was an experience. Days filled with group sessions regarding depression, and how to overcome it. But no one, not one of those "smart-assed-know-it-all doctors," could prescribe anything for my heartache. And that's just what it was — a heartache, in the worst way.

I took the medications which my psychiatrist, Dr. Bly, had prescribed and tried to follow the daily rules of the Psych Unit as best as I could. Fred, my husband, was very supportive during my month stay at the hospital. I guess if he would have had any idea, prior to our marriage, of the many times that he would enter this unit to visit me, maybe he would have thought twice about saying "I do."

After over a month of intense, psychological evaluations, and group therapy and drugs and God knows what else, I was finally released. Of course, there were no visible signs of change in my condition, but my doctors felt that I was no longer suicidal, and the depression, although it was yet there, was under control.

The cycle continued, however, and I was growing worse by the day. One night after remembering a terrible scene of incest with my father I found that life was no longer bearable and I decided to kill myself. I recall it as a "mercy killing." I was about to do what my father should have done to me years ago. He should have put me out of my misery and killed me. I guess that would have been too "good" of a thing for him to do.

Slowly I gathered together all the medications that I had been given at the hospital for my depression. There were bottles of junk that I didn't even know what they were to be used for. In spite of that, they were supposed to make me better. They failed. They didn't work. Nothing worked. Life hurt and I wanted the pain to stop. In retrospect, I can see how desperately I just wanted the pain to stop. If not forever, then just for a moment so that I could catch my breath.

Most of what occurred next is a blur to me. The ambulance, the paramedics, the tube down my throat, the stomach pump, it is now so obscure to me. Because of this "botched" suicide attempt I was hospitalized again because I was told by the attending nurse in the emergency room that "There is something severely and emotionally wrong with people who try to hurt or kill themselves."

"Shut-up," I wanted to say, to the doctor and nurses as they talked to Fred about me, as if I weren't even in the room. They handed him all the necessary papers to sign for my commitment into yet another hospital. And life went on.

chapter four

Somewhere between life, death, and incest there was Frederick, a gentle caring man who glided into my life on his "White Charger." I was fourteen years old when I met Fred at a roller skating rink. I thought when I saw him that he was the most handsome guy in the world!! It seems so long ago and so far away. . . .

I never felt that I was very pretty or that I had anything to be proud of, so I carried myself in sort of a nonchalant way. I didn't pay much attention to my hair, clothing or any of those things that my sisters took pride in. Regardless, Fred still seemed to like me. He was tall with beautiful "puppy-dog" eyes. I didn't know how I was going to bring myself to talk to him, but I knew that somehow I wasn't going to leave that roller skating rink until we at least said hello. My sister Ann was there with me. Ann was so much more outgoing than I was and had a lot of boyfriends. (She sneaked around so that my father wouldn't know about them.) At times, I hated her, but most of the time I just endured her cruelty towards me. Once, while walking down the street with her, she shoved me over onto the grass and yelled that she hated being seen with me because I walked like a retarded person.

Ann was two years older than I was, and she was tall and thin with a tiny little waistline and beautiful tan skin. I would watch her apply her makeup and secretly wish that I could be more like her. "Ann, why are you putting all that junk on your face?" I asked out of both jealousy and a genuine interest.

"So that my skin can stay beautiful and smooth, unlike yours, with all those pimples on it," she responded, as she wiped the skin cream from her face and continued on with her daily ritual. The whole bathroom smelled of Noxema and Ivory soap, and I thought if I stood there long enough that some of the steam that had been generated by the hot water would somehow affect my terrible acne. Everyone seemed to like Ann; she was a cheerleader at school and had so many friends. Everything seemed to come easy for her. She could put behind her everything that had gone on the night before at our house and act as if nothing was ever a problem.

"Are you just going to stand there and look at that boy roller skate, or are you going to go and talk to him?" Her question quickly brought my thoughts back to the rink, and to that good looking guy whom I wanted to meet.

"I'm going, Ann. Please don't embarrass me in front of all of these people," I said.

"I'm not embarrassing you. It's time for us to go and you've been staring at that boy all night, watching him roller skate. When are you going to ask him to skate with you?"

I took another look into the rink trying to locate this guy and sure enough he was looking right back at me. Suddenly he skated off of the floor and onto the carpeted area where we were standing and started toward me. "This is the last couples-only skate of the night. Would you like to skate it with me?" I couldn't believe it; I thought I was going to faint. He actually came over and spoke to me — he was asking me to skate.

"Of course she wants to skate." My sister's words rudely interrupted his talking. "Don't act like you haven't seen her staring at you all night," she said, so matter-of-factly.

"God, I hate her," I thought. I was so mad at her but yet her rudeness seemed to break the ice and we skated off towards the center of the rink. As we skated, the giant silver ball which hung above the rink began to twirl above us and sent off beautiful flickers of light with shiny sparkling slivers. The lights went dim, and I held onto Fred with my sweaty palms and prayed that I wouldn't fall or trip or be a "stupid klutz" as my sister had stated that I was.

Fred and I still talk about the first time we met. He brought something into my life that had been missing for a long time. He brought to me the fact that I might somehow be an all right person. Finding Fred, a person that I thought was so handsome, really seemed to give me a new high in life.

There were never any sexual overtones — we just really grew to like each other and he always seemed to be in tune as to how I was feeling. I could never fool Fred. If I had had an especially bad day at school, he would know — just by the sound of my voice on the telephone. For once, I felt that I had somebody who truly accepted me. I didn't have to worry about make-up and frilly hairstyles — he liked me just the way I was.

Dating wasn't allowed in our family although all my sisters did it secretly. Sometimes one of us would watch out of the back pantry window while the other one talked on the phone with her boyfriend. It was as if an "official lookout" was needed. While "looking out" one evening, I can recall seeing the tip of my father's car turning into the garage, and whispering, "Here he comes!" The phone suddenly clicked and everyone would run to their respective bedrooms. We didn't know if he was coming home drunk, sober, or just mean. Whatever his condition, if one of us were to be found on the telephone we would certainly get the beating of our lives. That was just the way it was done at our house. That was what we called normal. I knew that if I let out any hint that I had a boyfriend, and that if that information got out to my father, I would regret it.

I could never really explain to Fred about the random beatings that went on inside of the walls of the place I called home. We were friends and I just wanted to keep it that way. I was ashamed of my life and who I was. This was something new for him. He had never been exposed to any form of child abuse, and the closer we became, the more nervous I became.

I had completely blocked out the incest by the age of about thirteen and was now living with the physical abuse. I can now, however, as an adult recall how the incest stopped. My mother walked into her bedroom after work one day and found my father and me in bed together. Screaming filled the room; he told her that it was my fault; I was yelled at and sent off to my room. The next chain of events is unclear to me but my father somehow ended up at a rehabilitation center for what they were calling a "drinking problem." The matter was not discussed any further. My mother wanted him home, but for some reason someone else was calling the shots and he had to remain in that treatment center for quite some time. When he did return home, things were still the same — the only thing that was different was that he no longer called me into his room and memories of my knocking on his bedroom door were gone from my mind.

I felt that the whole turn of events was my fault. Our family had to live on food that other people gave us because my father was away locked up, and we received "gift" packages of clothing from the local church. My family was an outcast and for some reason I carried the guilt for what was happening to our family.

Thinking back to those times is really hard for me. I started to block out the incest, but I yet carried the guilt. The brain is a wonderful thing, with its protection mechanisms, and it allowed me, for my own protection, to store away in the deepest corner of my mind all the trauma which I had endured throughout my earlier childhood years.

One of the hardest times in my life came when all of my older sisters went off to college. They ran off to school as fast as they could and it left me paralyzed. It felt as if my life had been taken away from me. I didn't feel close to any of them, but having them there at home made me feel just a little bit safer. Slowly but surely, as I watched each of them, one by one pack their bags, I felt more doomed. I was now going to have to take on the responsibility of all of the cooking, cleaning and taking care of my mother, whose physical condition by this time was deteriorating. Muscular Dystrophy had overtaken her body and she could hardly move unassisted. Prior to this, we would all take turns taking care of her and it didn't seem like too much of a burden. I loved my mother, regardless of her condition, but her demanding tone sometimes made me want to walk away forever and never look back.

With my sisters gone, I found myself open again to my father's assaults. They were all physical with sexual overtones. There were times when he would hide behind my bedroom door and watch me undress and there were times that he would demand that I sleep with the door of my bedroom open, so that he could look at me. To me, this behavior was very intimidating. It made me very scared and uncomfortable but I didn't dare say anything to anyone because I felt so ashamed. Besides, whom was I going to tell and what would I say? "My father is a pervert and insists on peeking at me when I undress?" At the time, I didn't have a grasp or memory of my earlier years with this man.

Fred thought that I was the cat's meow, and as we grew older, he wanted that "official date." My heart stood still as he took control and demanded a meeting with my father. "If you don't come out and tell him about us, then I will," he said.

"But you don't know him; he might pull a gun on

you or something, or he might start beating me in front of you." My voice trailed off as I began to think of the many possible things that could go wrong.

"It's time for you to stop being afraid of your father and to stand up to him. If he touches you I'll kill him." At that moment I knew I would love Frederick Hughes Birts for the rest of my life. There had never been anybody who loved me enough to stand up to my father. Throughout all my life I had hoped and prayed for someone to come and help me and now here was this fifteen year old boy loving me and wanting to protect me.

"Fred," I finally said, trying to hold back the tears, "I love you."

He smiled and said, "I love you, too, peanut head."

Even though I dreaded it, I felt that maybe things would be okay if Fred spoke with my father, so he appeared at my front door requesting to speak to "Mr. Collins," and they sat down to talk. I could hear nothing. There were no bottles breaking or voices roaring. I heard nothing. Finally, I did hear the front door close, and I held my breath. Would he call me out and slap me? Would he break down my bedroom door? what? The back door slammed shut and I peeked out from the crack in my bedroom door. "He's gone; you can come out." My mother's voice was cold and distant.

"What happened?" I asked her slowly.

"Well, Fred told your daddy that he wanted to date you and he asked him if it would be all right if he stopped by the house to visit you from time to time, and your daddy said that it would be okay, on the weekends." That was it. The thing which I had feared most, seemed to be over . . . or was it?

"Juaniiiita!!!" His voice jumped out of the night like a sharp dagger piercing me through the heart. The sweat quickly beaded up on my forehead and I felt the life draining out of me. As I pulled my covers close to my chest, I prayed to God that He would take me. "Just take the life from my body and just allow me to die right now," I prayed. "Juaniiiita!!" His voice grew louder and louder as he threw the door to my bedroom open. "Get your goddamn ass out here and fix me something to eat!" I moved quickly, being careful to walk as fast as I could. The door to my mother's bedroom was partially open and I knew that she was awake, but not a sound came from her room. She never said a word. At that moment I truly hated my mother. I hated her for the weak woman that she was and would always be. I was a nervous wreck as I tried to warm his dinner. His cursing and stumbling around seemed more intense in my mind than most times, and as I reached for the skillet, I felt his hands pulling at my hair "You ain't nothing but a whore!, a bitch and a whore, just like your mama, she ain't nothing, and you ain't gonna ever be nothing!! I'm sick of you laying around on your ass doing nothing." His words went on forever and I stood there as he held my head back by my hair. The food was burning and I could smell the smoke but there was nothing to do. I wanted to scream out but he seemed to get so much satisfaction out of my crying, that I held it in. "You want a boyfriend, huh? Well, I'll be your boyfriend for you."

I can't recall if it was the pounding of his fist in my face, or the thrust of his foot into my stomach, but whatever the case, I lost my balance and hit the floor. I cried and pleaded with him to stop kicking me but he wouldn't. At this point, he seemed to grow angrier because his dinner was burning. "Get up I told you, bitch get up."

"Mama!" I cried, "Mama," but Mama just lay there in her bed. His drunken laughter filled the room.

"Your mama can't do nothing for you so I don't even know why you're calling her," he mused. I guess he was right, because that night I was beaten severely by my father and knocked down the basement steps only to be told to get back up and to finish making his dinner.

Somehow it had become clear to me as I wiped the tears from my face that either I was gonna have to die in this house from him beating me, or I would have to leave it. Leaving meant that I would turn my back on everything and end up on the streets. When I looked at my options, I knew that I had to find the strength to leave. He could kill me, shoot me, beat me; it no longer mattered. The pain that I had endured that night superseded any rational thought patterns that I might have had under any other circumstances and I slowly became a machine, moving almost robot-like through the house. I wiped the tears from my eyes, cut off the pot, and holding my stomach, slowly went into the pantry and opened the drawer that held the paper bags. I pulled a bag from the drawer and went to my room. I placed the contents of my top dresser drawer into the bag, and as my father stood by and watched in awe, I walked through the living room, opened the front door, and walked out into the night, the snow, and into the rest of my life.

chapter five

"Who in God's name is orchestrating my life!?" I thought, as I slushed through the snow. In my mind, and in my thoughts I immediately turned to that wonderful, safe family life which I sometimes conjured up, where I was sweet sixteen, lived in a quiet suburb, had lots of stupid teen-age parties, was carefree and where we played "twister" and talked about our boyfriends. It was always the same scene. Pretty girls in beautiful pink dresses at the "usual" slumber party. No cares, no torture, no pain . . . but somehow I couldn't maintain that facade tonight; I had to think about where I would go and how I would stay safe and alive. The little girl in me wanted desperately to run home to Mama, regardless, but the survivor in me knew that I couldn't. As I mounted the bus, I slipped my last fifty cents into the slot, and asked for a transfer. "This should give me time to think," I said, as I settled into my seat.

The tears wouldn't stop flowing and my nose was all stopped up. I kept looking for Daddy's car to pull up behind the bus. I kept waiting in fear, looking over my shoulders at every stop to see if he was following me. But he wasn't. I was all alone. The bus driver stopped the bus at an intersection and approached me. "Are you all right?" he asked.

"Yeah," I replied and pretended that I knew where I was going and that I had some real destination in my life. I finally thought of a friend, Carrie, who lived down the street from my house. We attended the same school and knew each other well. She sometimes stayed with her boyfriend, who was much older than we were. He had his own place, and I tried to recall its exact location. When I did remember, I got off of the bus and headed towards his house.

Jim looked at me as if I were a crazy person. "What the hell happened to you?" he asked as he opened the door. I was still holding my stomach and my eyes were red from crying.

"I ran away from home," I finally said, trying to hold back the tears. "Can I stay here with you for the night?"

He said nothing, but opened the door and took the garbage bag, which held my life's possessions. "I'll call Carrie," he said, and I sat timidly on the edge of the sofa, feeling both sick and exhausted from that night's activities.

The house was quiet and I could hear him talking on the telephone to Carrie. "She just showed up at my front door," I heard him saying. I always envied the relationship that Carrie and her mother shared. Her mother was an elderly woman who seemed so nice and easy to talk to. I would visit their home and just want to stay. It was just Carrie and her mom living together, and it always seemed so peaceful; they seemed to have a great relationship. She had so much freedom, and so much conversation went on between them. Jim was talking to Carrie's mom now, on the telephone, letting her know of the situation he was in and how he would feel more comfortable if Carrie came over that night to stay with me. "In the morning we can find a better arrangement," he said with a fatherly-sounding voice of concern. I couldn't help but feel like a stupid jerk. Here I was again, invading someone else's life with my problems.

I fell asleep on the sofa while Jim was gone to get Carrie. She arrived smiling and chipper, telling me that I had done the right thing. "Your daddy needs someone to kick his butt, just like he's been doing to you all of these years," Carrie said, as she walked through the front door.

"Yeah, that would be a funny thing to see," I said in response to her humorous remark. We talked most of the night and she really helped me to feel a lot better.

Fred came by later the next morning and when I saw him I could no longer hold back the tears. I just wanted him to hold me and tell me that everything would be all right. "We'll find some place for you to go. Jim said you could stay here as long as you need to."

I felt like an orphan, a child without a home, extra luggage. "I'll be fine," I said, trying to sound all grown-up.

Hours turned into days at Jim's and I no longer

wanted to impose, so I moved on. I felt that I had spent enough time imposing on him. After all, he wasn't my boyfriend; he was Carrie's. When Carrie couldn't be there things got a little bit uncomfortable with just the two of us. He meant well, but I was in no mood for conversation, and needed to be with people who didn't feel that they had to entertain me.

Beth was one of my closest friends. We were so much alike, and the differences which did exist between us just didn't seem to matter. Beth Fishbin was a spunky little redhead whose eyes dazzled and sparkled when she laughed. We met during our Freshman year at the school which we both attended in a nearby suburb which we referred to as "The Bay" (short for Whitefish Bay.) When she invited me to stay at her house, her mom insisted that my mother at least know where I was and that I was okay, so I called her. The conversation consisted of very little concern over my returning back home. I listened as she went on about my father and his threats to kill me if I ever did return. It seemed that she was holding back, or hiding something, as I listened to her voice on the phone. "Why don't you just come on out and say it Mama?" I said, bracing myself for whatever she had to say.

"Well," she finally said with great hesitancy, "I think that you would be safer where you are for right now. . . ." Her voice trailed off. She didn't ask me where I was, and she didn't want to know. She just wanted her life to be uninterrupted by an uproar over my coming back home. Now that I think about it, maybe she was right. She had been through enough. Why should she have to be subjected to watching me be beat to death by my father? When I hung up the telephone, I felt sick.

Beth's mom was stunned when she heard of my family situation. When I explained it all to her I felt both humiliated and embarrassed. "Your mother is under a great deal of stress and if she thinks that it's better for you not to return home, maybe you should listen to her."

Mrs. Fishbin told me of all of the wonderful foster homes that would just love to have me, and that if we went about this in the "proper" way, that I could continue to stay with them; however, she explained to me that for the sakes of everyone involved, that social services would eventually have to be notified. "Great," I said, "I can become a ward of the state!" I'm too old to be a foster child, I thought. I felt that there was something horrible about being surrounded by all of those rejected and abused children. Something about it left me feeling cold and empty inside. "Where was my real family? Where were my sisters?" I fumed to myself. I was sure that my mother had called them to tell them of this latest event. Where were they?

Better yet, where was she? I understood the workings of her illness, Muscular Dystrophy, yet I needed her. I needed her to intercede in some kind of way, but who was I kidding? "What are you gonna do?" Beth's voice interrupted my train of thought. I couldn't fool Beth; she knew me well. She knew everything about me. We were best friends. Sometimes I used to visit her and spend the night with her whenever my father took those famous trips to Mississippi to visit his mother. During my visits, we would run down the streets of "The Bay" during the late night hours. It was great!

So much peace. I never knew that it was possible to be so at peace with yourself, or your life. That's what it was always like with Beth, peace. We were the perfect odd couple. I was this scared little Black girl from a dysfunctional home, and she was a White Jewish Princess from the suburbs. We were two clowns. At school, we would do things that we knew would make people stare at us, like dressing alike, wearing our hair in the same hairdo. I think of the goofiest things we did, the one thing that we both seemed to like the most was when we would hold hands and dance as we sang "Billy Joel" hits down the corridors of our high school. ". . . Don't go changing, trying to please me, you never let me down before . . . ummmmm . . ." To this day, that song is still my favorite.

I loved Beth. I loved her like I have never loved another friend. She taught me so much about loving myself, and feeling good about who I was. She never looked down on me because I was black, because my parents weren't rich, or because we didn't live in "The Bay" like the rest of my snobby classmates . . . but most of all, I felt that Beth loved me. This got me through some rough times. Yet, I knew it would all one day end. Beth would leave me, or for whatever reason, we would part. But at that moment I needed to hold onto our good times.

"I know a Puerto Rican family from my old neighborhood and they agreed to let me stay with them," I said, wiping away the tears. "My mother said it was okay, and my father doesn't know. I'll be fine."

"You're getting real good at this packing up and leaving stuff," she said, handing me the rest of my clothes. "Here, don't forget this." I looked up and she was handing me my green jumper, which we had alike. We wore them on the days when we wanted to look like twins. "Thanks," I mumbled, as I stuffed the dress into my bag, feeling a giant knot forming in my throat. I wanted to grab her and to tell her that I loved her, and to make her promise that she would never leave me, to always stay in touch and . . . well, what did it matter? I felt after leaving their house that I needed to distance myself from such emotional feelings and outbursts. It seemed that whenever I loved someone, they would hurt me or leave me and I vowed to myself that this would never happen to me again. From then on, whenever I saw her in the hallways at school I would ditch her, or run into the girls' bathroom. I was too hurt to face her. I didn't want any friends; I didn't want her asking me questions, or asking me about my living arrangements.

I knew that she was worried about where I was living or if things had changed for me in any way, but those things were too painful to talk to her about. If this was what it felt like to care about someone, then I never wanted to get that close to another human being again — it hurt too much.

Once, when we finally did come in contact with each other, it was brief and I said I had to run. Later, I saw her with some other girls in the hallway and she waved to me. A rush of emotions overcame me and I felt extremely jealous. I felt that she should have been with me. That should have been us laughing and giggling in the halls . . . it just should have been . . . but I couldn't bring myself to face her. I was actually dodging the one person I longed to be with the most. Not only were we in separate classes now, but it seemed that we barely saw each other, and that's just what I wanted. I know my emotions contradicted my actions, but I didn't care. I told myself that I wanted to be left alone. I remembered the times when we would pick out our classes together to make sure we would be in the same rooms, but this semester things were different.

I knew that writing this book would be hard for me, and as I write about my friendship with Beth, I still feel pangs of guilt and sadness when I think about how the greatest friendship in the world ended. It was sudden and abrupt, like a gun shot. I finally stopped looking for her in the hallways. When I did see her, she was with someone else.

One day, I saw her sister, Linda, and asked her how Beth and her family were doing. What I received from her was a cold and distant reply. "Why don't you stop by the house tonight and see her? She's been sick for a long time and could probably use some cheering up."

"I never knew," I said to her in surprise. "What's the matter with her?"

"Just stop by, okay? Gotta run," she yelled, as she hurried off to her next class.

In my mind, I envisioned a million things but nothing prepared me for the shock which I received when I reached the top of her stairway and was heading into her bedroom. There she lay, completely immobilized in a body cast, her body frail and half its normal size. Her face was covered with acne and the room smelled damp and hospital-like. "What happened?" I finally asked, trying not to stare.

"I have scoliosis of the spine and the doctor said that the only thing I can do to correct my back, is to be put in a body cast for a year."

"A year?" I asked in disbelief.

"Yeah, bummer, huh?"

I looked around her bedroom. It didn't look like the same old joyful place that we used to talk in. Everything seemed to have changed. Instantly my mind, like a whirlwind, slapped me with memories of the dampness and coldness of my mother and her bedroom.

For years I had watched my mother confined mainly to her bed, yet battling to live a normal life. Everything that she needed or wanted seemed to come from me. The pressure of her illness was a great burden placed on me. When my sisters left home, not only did they leave me alone with my father, but they also left me alone to be both maid and nurse to my mother.

The visit with Beth was strained and uncomfortable, and I hated it. I hated that I had allowed my stupidity to ruin a perfectly good friendship, and I hated what had happened to Beth. "Could you pass me that silver bed pan?"

My face turned hot, and I began to feel like I was going to pass out. "Nooooo!" I screamed as I ran from her room and from her house. "This can't be happening, not again, and not to Beth."

I guess the bottom line was that I was afraid. Afraid that the one person in the world that I loved the most had somehow become just like my mother — sick and disabled.

After that visit with her, I refused to have anything else to do with her. The pain of it all was too much. I look back on my actions now, as the most misconstrued and selfish ones of my life. There was no explaining it. When I did finally get myself together, and tried to contact her, she wouldn't accept my calls. Her sister told me that she never wanted to speak to me again.

Even now, after years of growing, I still think of her with great pain. When I first got married I thought of her and would call all over town looking for her. I wanted finally to explain. I felt stronger. I was married and I wanted to talk to her. I wanted to tell her all about my life with Fred, and about my new baby. I wanted her in my life; I needed to explain. I found out finally that she was in college, in Madison, and so I wrote her long letters trying to explain, asking her to forgive me, but she never responded. After about ten years, I saw her sister in a local grocery store and asked her about Beth. She told me that Beth was now living in Milwaukee, so I began again to try and locate her. I called Directory Assistance and she was listed. My search was over. I had her telephone number right there in my hands!

I held tightly to the receiver as her telephone began to ring, and took in a deep breath. Her voice was soft, as she answered the phone. I told her who I was, and asked if we could get together. She said no, and the conversation ended abruptly. It still feels like a bad dream, like remembering the death of a loved one. A death that you never really quite get over.

chapter six

I have always loved the "Waltons." This was my favorite TV show. The closest I ever came to living this "ideal life" was when I moved in with the Felixes. While growing up, one of the greatest joys of my life was sitting in front of the television, watching The Waltons. Every Thursday night at seven p.m., while my mother went to choir rehearsal, that's where you could find me, watching the Waltons. Everything from Grandma Walton's baking to John Boy's writing became a part of me while I watched that show. I allowed myself to be completely engrossed, imagining how sweet the fields must have smelled or how delicious the breeze must have felt blowing down from "Walton's Mountain." Beautiful carefree children running in their overalls and saddle shoes. Never a care. Never a worry. Mama Walton would always be in the kitchen creating a simple but delicious meal for dinner, complete with her home-made blueberry pie. Papa Walton would be in the back yard hammering away or fixing things. It didn't have to be anything important. Once, he was constructing a beautiful doll house that he had spent most of the summer working on as a surprise birthday present for his youngest daughter, Elizabeth. Yeah, that was my favorite episode.

I would sit on the dirty living room floor, oblivious of my surroundings, and study every detail of their utopian lifestyle. Every pain endured by that family became my pain; their joys became my joy. Even visiting with the "Baldwin Sisters," with their papa's "secret recipe" was wonderful to me. It all seemed so lovely. At the end of the program I would always sit there in tears, clutching my tissue, listening to all their good nights. "Good night Ben" . . . "Good night John Boy" . . . "Good night Sue Ellen, Elizabeth, Jason, Mary Ellen, Grandma" . . . I wanted it to go on forever! At the end of the show I'd listen to the soft theme music, cry, and then it would all be over, gone, ka-putz! As I grew older and more cynical, I thought, as I watched this program, that a disclaimer should appear at the on-set of this show (for the mentally unstable) saying something like **"Warning! Warning! Attention all morons, this program is not real, and if taken too seriously, it could be mentally damaging to your health, as you try to make the transition back from fantasy, to the cruel realities of your own sorry and miserable lives. . . ."**

Life with the Felixes wasn't like living on "Walton's Mountain," but it was a loving and warm household. Carlos was an older Spanish man with strong family ties and he owned his own grocery store located right next to their home. His wife

Norma was fifteen years his junior. She was easy to talk to and we got along just fine. I first met the family when I was about ten years old, before my family moved away from that neighborhood. Things were so different back then. During my childhood, my family lived in the house which Carlos and Norma now owned and were living in. The Felixes at that time lived next door above their store. As a little girl, I was really fascinated by the thought of owning your own candy store and quickly made friends with this Puerto Rican family. I liked the strange way in which they spoke and found myself hanging around the store whenever my father wasn't around. It didn't seem to bother them; in fact, they seemed to really like me. Sometimes their little girls would run around the store playing tag or eating candy. We would all wait around to hear one of Carlos' stories of the "old country" and life in Puerto Rico. Their family didn't have an abundance of money but they really loved each other and that was something which my life seemed to be missing.

During the summer, I would spend my days in the store sitting on top of old crates, drinking grape sodas and helping Carlos to wait on his customers. The store was filled with good things to eat and the meat in the back meat cooler smelled of delicious Spanish spices and fresh garlic.

Looking back, I guess one of the most special things about our relationship was that it made me feel like I belonged. I felt like someone loved me and cared about me. Sadness fills my heart when I recall how empty and needy a child I must have appeared to be.

My father, of course, hated that I spent so much time with them. I guess he was worried that people would find out about some of the abuse that was going on in our house. There were times that I had to sneak out the back door of the store when his car pulled up. Right away, all the pain would return to me when I would see that yellow Cadillac slowly ease into the open space in front of our house. Seeing his car evoked a great fear from within me. It meant that "Daddy" was home from work, and there was no telling how drunk or abusive he would be that night. I'm sure, looking back, and from what they now tell me, that Carlos and Norma actually did hear quite a bit of the violence that erupted from our house. Felixes' Grocery Store was so close to our house that in the summertime when the windows were open anyone around could hear all the fighting going on from within our house.

After our family moved away from East Lloyd St., I tried to keep in touch with my "other family," but life was so filled with pain that having a healthy relationship with healthy people was very hard for me. So, when I decided to leave Beth and move in with them as their foster daughter, I was both happy and sad. I was sad because it was something that I wanted so badly as a child, but now as a teenager, I felt like used luggage, being pulled and dragged around and dumped off in "no-man's land."

When Carlos heard of my plight he insisted that I have a decent place to live and made arrangements to have me come and stay with them. Even though I knew these people well, there was still an uneasy feeling in the pit of my stomach when I moved in. I tried very hard to fit into their family and not to cause too much trouble.

It was hard to go back to a place where so much physical violence had taken place. As I walked through the house I could feel the tears swelling up in my eyes. The flashbacks of children wailing and pleading not to be beaten brought it all back to me and I wanted to run and hide. I was filled not only with hurt and pain but shame. The shame of my childhood was gnawing at my heart. The only comfort that I could find was from within myself. Somehow I reached deep within and told myself that "The beatings are over, you're safe, there is nothing to be ashamed of — it wasn't your fault." I truly loved these people and wanted this new living arrangement to work out. I was tired of being tossed around and after having lived through so much pain and heartache I had become very numb. I felt as if I was walking around in a daze. I always thought that I could handle a lot, but somehow I felt that all of my resources had been tapped. I had nothing left and could barely feel.

I lived with this foster family until the end of my seventeenth year. I learned more about real family life than any "Waltons" episode could have ever portrayed. There were many sleepless nights and outbursts of anger and yes, I did try to get my way, but I was firmly and gently shown that some of my behaviors would not be tolerated. Frederick was allowed to come by from time to time; however, even that wasn't enough to bring me out of my shell. It was as if I had gone into hiding emotionally. The walls which I had erected to protect me from pain were hard to penetrate.

I didn't see much of my mother throughout this time. She had hired a nurse to come by daily to attend to her needs and when I asked her if I could stop by, she would always tell me that it was a bad idea. I can recall hanging on tightly to the telephone receiver wanting desperately to hear her say that she loved me and wanted me to come home but she never did. Mama never in her life told me that she loved me, or that she was sorry for what I was going through. It was as if she didn't even care. Not having my mother to talk to or any of my real family members around left me feeling very rejected and insecure. I was constantly thinking that there was something terribly wrong with me. As my senior year in high school was coming to an end, I tried very hard to make good grades. I was unsure about my life. I wanted to go to college but it seemed so incomprehensible. How in the world could I ask people who weren't even related to me to send me to college?

Through all of my ups and downs, Fred never left me. He was always there by my side. He seemed to understand every feeling that I had. I never had to try and impress him; he said that he just loved me and wanted to spend the rest of his life taking care of me and being my husband. Being married and finally having a place of my very own to call home was both a scary thought and a wonderful dream.

Frederick was eighteen years old when he proposed to me and I was seventeen. I wasn't of age but I had a birthday coming up, so I began to plan for my wedding. My mind became a playground filled with dancing images of the "perfect wedding." I imagined magnificent colors and scenery. White bows draping sensuously around the pulpit. Rose petals sprinkled lavishly down the center aisle of a towering cathedral with guests jam-packed within the church (due, of course, to the crowd's overwhelming turnout for this "social event of the decade"). And of course, there would be the bride. I would appear out of my private dressing room, like a ubiquitous Goddess, wearing a gown made of only the finest imported silk and lace. My bouquet, flown in from Paris, of course, would consist of white roses, lilies and just a hint of baby's breath. After our wedding vows were exchanged, my handsome Prince and I would make our royal exit to our chauffeured carriage, led by six of the most beautiful Arabian white horses, and we would trot off into the sunset living happily ever after.

The reality of my life, however, was that there really wasn't much money for such frivolous luxuries. There was only the money that I had managed to save while working after school at a Walgreens, and the money which Fred had saved from his job as a waiter.

After the dust clouds passed, and reality finally set in, Norma and I worked hard on a simple wedding plan. Fairytales were out of the question, and the only thing that mattered to me at that time was that I was going to marry the one and only person that truly loved me and cared about me.

During this time, in the state of Wisconsin, the laws stipulated that if a couple wanted to marry, they both had to have blood tests. There was a seven-day waiting period in which they either had to be of legal age, or if not, both parents of those applying had to sign in order for the wedding to take place.

This problem began to become very real to me after I realized that we had set a wedding date of June 2nd, and in order for me even to apply for a license I would have to be eighteen years old at least seven days prior to my applying for the marriage license. The only way around this big mess would be to go to my natural parents and ask them to sign a legal document agreeing to allow me to marry. Of course, this was when everything began to fall apart.

I was again at the mercy of my father, a man who despised me greatly and whose only joy it seemed in life was hurting others. My father's response was a sharp no. "I'm not gonna sign nothing for you. You ran off to live with those damn Puerto Ricans, well, let them try to sign for you and see how far you'll get. I'm your daddy and don't you ever forget it!!"

The tears filled my eyes as I began to cancel my wedding plans. "That's just like him," I raged, as I wiped away the tears which were by now streaming down my face. "His last chance to screw up my life and of course, he has to take it."

"What are we gonna do?" I asked Fred.

"Well, don't worry about it; we'll wait until you're eighteen and then file the papers."

"But if I wait until I'm eighteen and file, that won't be in time enough for the wedding."

"Then, I guess we'll just have to wait until your eighteenth birthday, regardless."

It seemed so simple the way Fred put it. He refused to allow things to upset him or me. We often joked that he was my "Prince Charming," and he really was. We arrived at the County Courthouse on my birthday and appeared before the judge. We calmly explained our situation to him. The judge took a long hard look at us, asked us a few questions and within two hours we left the courthouse, on Thursday, May 31st, 1979, as Mr. and Mrs. Birts.

"Marriage is something which should not be entered into lightly. . . ." I remember the chaplain's words quite clearly. Those first few years were filled with a lot of turbulence and sometimes I didn't know if we were going to make it together. The best thing that we had going for us was that we were best friends. Even though it has now been twelve years, our marriage is yet changing. Every since Fred has known me, I have suffered with depression. I floated in and out of it throughout our courtship, but it seemed to be magnified a hundred times its size after our marriage.

I really wanted to be happy and to be a good wife to Fred, but my emotions were completely out of whack. Some days I could barely find enough strength to crawl out of bed. When I did finally get up, I cried all day long. After the birth of our second child, my life was completely out of control. My very desire to live had diminished. I had two beautiful children whom I loved dearly, yet that wasn't enough. The depression was growing and roaring within me like a woman in travail with child.

chapter seven

When feelings of suicide and utter despair overwhelmed me, I cried out for help to the two doctors whom I had been dealing with for the past two years of my depression. When I first met Dr. Bly and Dr. Warner, in 1988, I didn't really want to cling to them for my psychiatric stability, but I found that I was in constant contact with both of them during my days of despondency.

I hated that I appeared to be so needy, so out of control and so overwhelmed. I wanted to attack this depression thing and cure it like one would the "common cold." I read stories all of the time about people with incurable diseases, who would search the world over for some type of miracle drug, so that they could continue on with their lives. In my current situation, I felt like one of those people. I had very little support from my family regarding another hospitalization, but similar to the person with cancer, or any other life-altering sickness, I wanted my life back!! I wanted to wake up in the morning and hear the birds sing and bask in the warmth of the sun and not to feel the gutter-level drudge of my never-ending depression sapping the life from my body. Was this too unreasonable? How could anyone begrudge me this simple desire?

Throughout my many visits to my doctors and my therapist, I had been told by people who were supposed to be supporting me, that I was merely a "doctor junkie," going from one doctor to another, searching like a fool for that magical pill that was going to cure me. Maybe a part of this scenario was true, but I have found that for every person alive, there is an opinion, and people have no problem imposing their opinions upon anyone vulnerable enough to embrace them.

It was at this time that I turned to my Higher Power for strength and picked up my Bible to read of the sufferings of my dear friend, Job. His pain somehow helps me to keep a perspective on my own condition. It affirms within me that there is hope. Parallel to me, Job both loved and respected his Higher Power, and stood in awe of his miraculous Deity. Nevertheless, when he was driven to the brink — that last straw, his sufferings pose as a testimony to the fact that even the best of us at one time or another in our lives have actually questioned God and our place in this vast Universe. My favorite part of the story comes towards the end, when all of Job's friends and family had either left him or were all dead and he lay withering in pain feeling that all hope was gone. It was at this miraculous time that God restored him both physically and emotionally. So, yes, I do in my time of pain turn to the words spoken by a very wise and long-suffering man.

> *"I am weary of living. Let me complain freely. I will speak in my sorrow and bitterness. I will say to God, 'Don't just condemn me — tell me why you are doing it. Does it really seem right to you to oppress and despise me, a man you have made; and to send joy and prosperity to the wicked? Are you unjust like men? Is your life so short that you must hound me for sins you know full well I've not committed? Is it because you know no one can save me from your hand?' . . . You have made me, and yet you destroy me. Oh, please remember that I'm made of dust — will you change me back again to dust so soon? You have already poured me from bottle to bottle like milk, and curdled me like cheese . . . You gave me life and were so kind and loving to me, and I was preserved by your care. . . . Now, I am filled with frustration. . . . Why then did you even let me be born? Why didn't you let me die at birth? Then I would have been spared this miserable existence. I would have gone directly from the womb to the grave. . . . My complaint today is still a bitter one, and my punishment far more severe than my fault deserves. Oh, that I knew where to find God — that I could go to his throne and talk with him there. I would tell him all about my side of this argument, and listen to his reply, and understand what he wants. Would he merely overpower me with his greatness? No. He would listen with sympathy. Fair*

> *and honest men could reason with him, and be acquitted by my judge. . . . But I search in vain. I seek him here, I seek him there, and cannot find him. I seek him in his workshop in the North, but cannot find him there; nor can I find him in the South; there, too, he hides himself. But he knows every detail of what is happening to me; and when he has examined me, he will pronounce me completely innocent — as pure as solid gold!!"*

I was humiliated over the idea of entering again into the hospital. "We're talking ten days at the most, Briéanna," Dr. Bly assured me. "We just need to regulate your medication so that you can begin to function again at a more stable level." I guess sleeping until three o'clock in the afternoon wasn't considered a "normal existence." Neither were the constant struggles with suicide, so after much reluctance and after talking it over in great detail with both Fred and Michael, I pulled my tail between my legs like a wounded and defeated puppy and submitted to this decision.

It was the beginning of October, the weather was just beginning to turn brisk, the pears in my back yard were ripe and falling like rain to the ground, and I felt like crap! Just thinking about going back into the hospital left me feeling numb. How could I explain to my children that "Mommy is going back into the hospital for another medication change?" But somehow I had to, I had to get through it.

"Maggie," one of the unit's counselors, met me at the admissions desk full of smiles. She was the sweetest woman that I had met in quite some time. I remembered her clearly from my previous stays at this hospital, and felt that she was one of the reasons that I was able to make it through those hard times. She would always come into my room and sit and talk with me. She made me feel that I was important, and that allowed my pain to be validated. Most of the people that I had come in contact with and that I tried to share my pain with just weren't able to deal with it. They listened for a while and then I got this same response — "That was a long time ago, forgive, get on with the rest of your life." If they didn't all say the same thing, it sure sounded that way to me. What little hope or empathy that was given to me always ended with my "Getting on with the rest of my life," or "Putting the past behind me."

Maggie always had something positive and warm to say, and she tried, during the long ride up on the elevator, to make me feel comfortable. As we carried my belongings up to my room, I felt like both a failure and a moron. I felt that my returning to this hospital unit somehow meant that I was weak and couldn't make it out in the "real world." I felt defeated and that all of my previous hospitalizations had been in vain. Everything on the ward still looked the same. The stale and obscure portraits which hung on the walls were yet there, giving off the illusion of warmth. But, I knew better. All the same nurses and unit clerks spoke to me as I passed from one side of the ward to my designated area to join the rest of the "sick-os" and the severely depressed.

I received my own private little room and brought in things from home that were supposed to make me feel better. I unpacked and tried to prepare myself for what I thought would be a ten day stay at this hospital. A test called a "QEEG," which is supposed to monitor brain waves and determine the status of a person's depression, had been given to me prior to my check-in date. The results of this test indicated that my depression was severe and resistant to traditional types of treatments. After having considered these results, Dr. Bly decided that a certain drug called "Nardil" would be the drug of choice for this visit. I had tried it before but had terrible urinary retention, and had to be taken off of it after a horrible time with catheters and infections. "This time would be different," Dr. Bly assured me. There was a drug available called Urecholine which would be used to counter-act the effects of the Nardil on my bladder, thus deleting the possibilities of urinary retention. Like most things in my life, that plan just didn't work for me. The bladder stimulant failed to stop the urinary retention and before I knew it, I was caught up in a vicious cycle of being catheterized on a daily basis.

I found the inability to have my urinary system function normally depressing beyond words. There were times that I would just sit on the toilet and pray to urinate. "Oh God just let it flow, if not a lot, then just a little, just enough to relieve my bladder." Dr. Bly was apprised of this travesty and quickly took me off the Nardil and placed me on another antidepressant called Anafranil, which he said would be better for my bladder. This drug, however, proved to be worse than the first one in terms of urinary retention, and the catheterization process began all over again. This time around, the urinary retention was accompanied by a urinary tract infection, which in turn led to a terrible bladder infection. I went to great pains to research each new drug that I was placed on — I almost felt like a chemist. I wanted to know everything about any drug that I would be ingesting and its side effects. With all of the problems that I was experiencing, it became very evident to me, as time passed by, that any possibility of being released from this hospital was far from sight.

The frequent catheterizations were cited for my infections. The thought of being catheterized was at the bottom of my list of "neat" things to do while in the hospital. However, one quiet night, after having tried for numerous hours to eliminate on my own, I gave in to the cold hard facts that I was going to have to have a nurse come into my room and catheterize me. The very thought of it made me ill. It was a cold and humiliating process, where I lay with my legs open for all the world to see, and have some person, whom I didn't know, shove a tube through my urethra and drain urine from my body. What a thrill!! Yet, I had no choice. It was either that or die of some sort of a urine back-up, so I rang in desperation for the unit nurse to bring the catheterization equipment to relieve me. I crawled to the cord and rang for help. After my emergency light had been on for over ten minutes with no response, I tried again. I could barely walk because of the distention of my bladder, and lay limply in pain waiting for the nurse who never came. Instead, Maggie, who was in the middle of one of her counseling groups, came. She had become irritated by the constant ringing of the emergency bell and decided to investigate. What she found was my body limply hovering over the bed in pain, begging to be relieved and she quickly ran to get the unit nurse who was supposed to be on duty that night.

"What is the problem?" was the nurse's reply. "Why can't a grown woman like you get up and walk to the bathroom? Why do you need my assistance?" Maggie stood by and listened in horror at the barrage of questions being hurled at me. "Turn over and let me feel how distended your bladder is," the male nurse ordered, very coldly. By this time, my body was perspiring profusely and I had the shakes. I couldn't stand the pressure on my bladder, and answering the questions which he was throwing at me was both demeaning and agonizing.

"I'm having urinary retention due to the medications," I managed to reply as I winced in pain. "It's all in my chart. Please, can you hurry?" I begged this nurse, "Help me." The nurse very coldly responded that he would "check into it," and left the room. Maggie had to get back to her group, so she apologized to me for this nurse's abrupt behavior, and assured me that she would be back to check on me shortly. After another thirty-five minutes had passed, I slipped to the floor and crawled to the bathroom to try just one more time. "Please God," I prayed, "Just a little, just allow me a little relief." But nothing passed. I felt like an over-blown balloon that would bust at any second. I was hyperventilating, sweating and going through what felt like a million stages of unconsciousness. My legs were numb and my fingers trembled as I tugged at the emergency light above the toilet, which sent a bellowing alarm out to the nurses' station.

The nurse arrived at my bathroom door, and without opening it to check on my condition, he said to me in his formidable and rigid voice, "Briéanna, please don't ring that bell anymore. I'm aware of your situation. I told you I was checking your chart and your constant ringing of that bell is interrupting my work."

"I'm sick, please help me, I feel like I'm going to bust," I cried — but he was gone. I felt at that moment that I truly was going to die. I felt that my internal organs were about to erupt and that I was either going to throw up these organs orally or that they were all going to erupt internally and I would die. "Get a grip on yourself, Briéanna," I instructed myself. I focused on the door and prayed for the strength to crawl towards it. Without regard to the fact that I was naked from the waist down, I lowered my body onto the cold bathroom tile and crawled on my hands and knees to the hallway. It felt as if the doorway was getting farther and farther away, that the room was getting larger and larger, but I finally made it out into the hallway and onto the carpet. With all the strength and fiber of my being I reached down and found my voice. "Help! Help! Somebody help me, help me!" At that moment every patient on the floor emerged from his or her room or group meeting and ran to my assistance. They picked me up from the floor and carried me to my bed, while another patient ran to another area of the hospital and returned with a nurse and a catheter kit.

I was in bad shape. All I could say to the nurse

attempting to help me was "Thank you." She placed cold towels on my forehead and began to talk very quietly and soothingly to me telling me to take in deep breaths and to slow down my breathing. She seemed very angry at the nurse who was on duty that night and exchanged words with him that I couldn't make out, but finally I did hear her ask him to leave the room. I welcomed the catheter, the cold cleansing towels, which were used to prep my body for the insertion of the catheter, I welcomed everything!! I just wanted relief. At this point the entire floor was in an uproar over what they had just experienced and had to be calmed down. What my bladder had retained was sixteen hundred units of urine. The nurse from the other unit made note of this parody and called for the head of the nursing staff, who came up immediately to see what had happened.

    She also took down other complaints that the residing patients had regarding the quality of care being given on the floor which we were on. That experience left me feeling so disregarded and disposable. The following morning everyone involved of course had to give a statement of what they had observed the night before to the Administration Staff.

chapter eight

As a direct result of both staff complaints and the patient's statements given to the Administrative Board the next morning, regarding Nurse Kelly's blatant neglect and irresponsibility, his employment was immediately terminated.

"Why, God?" I asked in my moments of sanity. "What could I have ever done in my life to deserve such treatment?" What had started out as a ten-day medication change had turned into a "Hospital stay from hell." The weeks had passed, Halloween had come and gone and I was still in the hospital looking at the reality that I might be lying in this same bed come Thanksgiving Day. The whole escapade was causing an enormous strain on Fred and the kids, so I quickly set up a therapy session for the children, with Michael. I had now been hospitalized for two months, and my children wanted their mommy back home.

Because of this ordeal with Nurse David Kelly, after his termination, an IVP test was ordered by

Dr. Bly. It was to determine if there were any damages sustained to my bladder due to his neglect. I was trying to be the perfect patient, which under the circumstances wasn't very easy, so when I began to have pelvic pain a few days later, I put off talking about it to my doctor for as long as I could.

Finally, I realized that there was something wrong and I needed to see a gynecologist. I complained constantly of pelvic pain and Dr. Bly ordered a gynecologist to be sent in to examine me. Throughout the pelvic exam, this doctor of gynecology made a few grunts and murmured a few inauspicious comments to his nurse about "possible fibroids," but never entered into a dialogue with me regarding his findings or my condition. When I asked him what he had found, he said, "You're fine, nothing to worry about."

"But didn't I hear you say something about my having fibroid tumors?" I asked him. It was like trying to get blood from a turnip, to get this guy to give me a straight answer.

"Well, I said **Possible**. There's nothing to get upset about."

The fact of the matter was that I <u>was</u> upset! I was angry at everything and everybody! "How could a doctor, whom I'm paying, examine me and not talk to me?" I raged to myself. "Fibroids may not be a big issue to you, but they certainly are to me," I responded to this doctor who was by now on his way out of the examining room. After he left, all I could think about was the year of 1985, when I had a fibroid tumor that was "Not to be taken too seriously" and the darn thing grew to the size of a grapefruit, and had by then connected itself to one of my Fallopian tubes and an ovary. So, consequently, this man saying to me "Not to worry" was ludicrous!!

I was placed on medication for my bladder infection, which seemed to persist, and taken off all antidepressants — and yes, I was a wreck. One nurse was nice enough to share the IVP results with me. The tests showed that there were no visible signs of damage to either my bladder or kidneys, yet there was something "strange" appearing on the test, and that was my uterus. It seemed that my uterus was extremely enlarged, and pressing on my bladder. I discussed this with the nurse on duty that night and told her that I had had enough!!

"I came to this hospital for a med change. I'm on no antidepressants, my bladder is killing me and I'm a mess!! I have a urinary tract infection, and a staff gynecologist tells me in passing that, 'Oh yes, by the way, you have fibroid tumors, but not to worry!!' What kind of hospital is this?" I screamed.

The fact of the matter was that I wasn't eating, I wasn't sleeping and the pain in my body was debilitating. Later that night, the pain in my side had become so excruciating that it was intolerable. I slowly walked to the nurses' station and asked for pain medication. I was told that the medication which I was requesting (a pain pill) had not been ordered by my doctor and that there was nothing that she could give me. The nurse also told me in an "ever-so-gentle-manner" that it was too late to put a call through to my doctor, "Just for a pain pill."

Immersed in rage, I slowly turned away from her (for fear of what I might do to her pretty little face) and without a word, I headed towards the telephone in the hallway and placed the call to Dr. Bly's office for myself. The answering service, which took my initial call, contacted John, who was Dr. Bly's Personal Assistant and I was told that he would return my call. I sat in the hallway, perched in a chair against the wall right next to the telephone, waiting in desperation for John's return call. When he finally did contact me, I informed him of my pain, my discomfort and the reason for my call.

"John," I spoke slowly, and deliberately, "You know what I've been through, and if I don't get some kind of pain pill soon, I don't know what I'm going to do." John assured me that he would call in my order for medication to the nursing staff and that I would get some relief that night.

I didn't care at that point what the nurses thought of me. I had been referred to many times before during my stay at this hospital as the "Queen Bitch" because I had made my needs known to both the staff and my doctors. If expressing my needs was grounds for this insignia, then I was content to wear it without apology. I felt like a woman whose rights and human dignity had been taken away.

After I hung up the receiver from talking to John, I began to explore my options, and questioned whether I had made a wise decision in returning to this hospital. The nurse, Lucy, walked out into the hallway waiting for some kind of response from me regarding John's call. "Well?" she asked, sarcastically.

"John will be calling you with orders for a pain pill," I replied and limped off to my room.

I lay shaking and trembling in bed, my face saturated with sweat, when the door of my room was flung open. "John said that this is all you can have until tomorrow." This nurse handed me two little white pills which I quickly reached for with my frail and quivering hands. Never did this nurse acknowledge my trembling or my pain.

My pain in fact was so bad that after taking the pills, a swarm of nausea hit me and I began to throw up uncontrollably. I could hardly lift my head from the pillow, and vomit spumed across the room and down the side of the bed. When Lucy returned to do her usual bed check, not only did she find me half unconscious, but she also found me lying in a puddle of regurgitation. I was yet experiencing a "gag effect" from throwing up, when out of nowhere she began to scream and yell at me about "making it to the bathroom."

"You could have made it to the bathroom. Who do you think is going to clean this up? I'm not. There's a waste paper basket over there in the corner; you could have used that!!"

This situation, regardless of the fact that it was happening to me, was playing out like some sort of a tragic comedy. There I lay, with a urinary tract infection, a bladder infection, but I was supposed to "leap like a frog" to the bathroom so as not to disrupt this nurse's evening!! God forbid that she, a nurse, should have to clean up my bodily fluids!

"Forgive me," I whispered, as I tried to lift my head from the puddle of vomit which my face was lying in. "The last thing that I would want to do is to inconvenience you in any way by having you clean up after me." Lucy stormed out of the room only to return with cleaning materials and began to wipe away at the surface vomit but stated that

"Housekeeping would have to do the rest tomorrow." (Meaning, changing the sheets, of course.)

So, there I lay, immobilized, and inhaling the remnants of my vomit. Feeling as low as a snake's belly, I took a deep breath and with the little bit of dignity that I was able to muster up, I pulled myself together and out of that bed, and at three o'clock in the morning, I began to pack my clothes — I was going home.

I did realize that I wasn't on a medical unit of this hospital, and that this was a floor for individuals with emotional and behavioral problems, but my situation had been quickly turned from an emotional ordeal to that of a physical one, which at that moment was taking precedence over everything else that was going on with me emotionally. I didn't feel like being rational, or thinking intellectually; all of that had gone. I wanted one thing, and that was to go home. I knew that I could hardly walk. The aching in my back impaired both my walking and my standing, yet I wanted to go home! Fred would help me. He would take care of me. As I wiped the tears from my eyes, I began to pack my clothes into a small tote bag.

"I can check into an emergency room of any local hospital and find some sort of medical attention," I thought, as I tried to convince myself that I was doing the right thing.

"Where do you think you're going?" Lucy, the nurse, asked me.

I braced myself against the door of my room and said in a matter-of-fact voice, "I'm going home."

I appeared at the nurses' station with my coat and hat on and announced that I was discharging myself. I stood there waiting for the appropriate papers to be given to me so that I could sign them. Instead, the nurse reached for the telephone and called my doctor.

Given the lateness of the hour and the condition that I was in, my doctor refused to discharge me. He stated that I was too sick to leave, and that my choices were either to be injected with some drug (in the posterior) to calm me down, or if I continued to stand there demanding to be released that security would be called and I would be carried away into isolation.

After hearing my options, I slowly placed my bag on the floor and sat huddled in the corner in utter amazement and pain. I regressed in my mind to the time of my childhood when I would be told "No" — just because, and dared to question why. Things didn't have to make sense back then; I was the child and they were the parents. That's how I was feeling this night. Somehow I had regressed back into that same familiar child-like state and had relinquished all of my power to my "Parents" (who at this time were the doctors and the nurses of this unit). I felt that small, insignificant, abused child emerging — helpless and devoid of any direction or any tangible sense of herself. The metamorphosis created here was that of a woman-turned child-turned time bomb.

It began to dawn on me that my life (or this tragic comedy) had become an almost hysterical, satirical irony, and it hit me with such a jolt that I began to laugh aloud. I must have looked like a neurotic fool, sitting there on that floor half laughing and half crying.

Shortly after my refusal to get up off of the floor and to return back to my room like a "Good little girl," a security guard, accompanied by one of the city's police officers, appeared before me demanding that I either "Go off quietly to my room" and allow the nurse to inject me with this "nice" medication, or, if I continued to sit there, they were going to haul me off into isolation.

"You mean to tell me that I can't leave this hospital on my own accord, when I checked in here two months ago on my own? Why?" I screamed as loud as I could. At this point I didn't care about the time, or waking other patients. I wanted this nightmare to be over.

"That's right," the officer replied. "We have no more time to deal with your temperament. Which one will it be?"

"Take me to isolation," I finally said. Before I could get the words out of my mouth these robust guys were pulling me up to my feet and I flinched in pain. "I said I would go into isolation!!" I pronounced, trying not to cry, yet losing my fight of holding back the tears. "You don't have to bully me; I have a bladder infection and I can barely walk. You don't have to treat me like a hardened criminal."

"Yeah, go easy, she does have a bladder infection," the nurse finally said in my defense. "Thank God for small favors," I thought.

Isolation was a cold room with a single mattress thrown in the middle of the floor, bare walls and bright lights beaming down from the ceiling. Before entering isolation, I was searched, stripped of my shoes and all of my belongings and was left with only my sweat shirt, socks and my jeans. I huddled in a corner, as "someone" watched my every motion through a two-way mirror. "Don't let them see you cry, Brié, don't," I told myself, as I clutched at the pain on the left side of my body. "Maybe this situation really isn't so bad. Maybe I really can get through this night," I told myself over and over again. "Everything will be all right in the morning."

In the morning, I would once again return to my room and be able to have my "Pooh Bear" and smash my tired and miserable face into the softness of his fur. He would understand; I could always tell Pooh everything. Then, Fred will come to help me. "Yeah, things are always better in the morning. This will all seem like just another one of my bad dreams," I said, trying to comfort myself as I rocked back and forth on the hard mattress. "This isn't so bad. . . ."

As time passed in isolation, a nurse whom I had never seen on the unit before unlocked the door of the isolation room and spoke to me in a soft and soothing voice. "You know, you don't have to stay here in the cold. The medication which your doctor has ordered for you will really make you feel a lot better and take away some of that pain which you're having. I've been watching you. You need to be in your own room in your own bed tonight, and not on this cold hard floor." As she spoke I began to cry softly; I felt that I had lost all control of my life and my reasoning.

"But the nurse wants to stick me with a needle and I'm afraid of needles," I said, wiping my nose with the back of my shirt sleeve. Suddenly I could no longer hold back the tears and began to sob with intense agony while this nurse held me in her arms. I cried and cried until I felt that there was nothing left. I was crying about all of the injustices which I felt had been thrust upon me. I cried over all the flashbacks which I had been having, replete with those horrible memories of abuse, I cried over all of the needles that I had endured, all the tests, all the exams, but most of all I cried hardest about those damn catheters and the loss of my dignity which I felt that the procedure left me with. Each time a catheter had to be inserted into me, it felt like yet another violation upon my body. I fought in my mind with feelings of being both raped and molested, all over again. I was also trying to fight off the strong feelings of being a child again, coming under submission to my father's control. So, I cried some more. I cried until it felt as though all of the burdens ever placed upon me had been lifted.

Finally after allowing me to regress and let down my guard, the nurse said in a motherly tone, "I'll talk you through it. The medication in this needle will really help to ease some of that pain in your side. I know it might hurt a bit, but it will make you feel much better. . . ."

As she spoke, another nurse from a different ward, whom I had met several times, appeared beside me and sat down on the floor and held my hands. The pain was very intense as she injected me with the needle. There also was a strong, burning sensation afterwards, but relief did seem to come immediately. I decided to stay on my own accord in the isolation room that night because I didn't think that I could stand the thought of going back to my assigned unit and having to look at Lucy. I just didn't want to be reminded of any of the things which she had put me through that night.

"Briéanna, I've come to take you home." Her voice sounded like that of an angel. I looked up and there stood the head nurse of the day shift. She had come to take me back to my room. Along with her was Michael. I know that I must have looked as if I had just been run over by a train, but it didn't matter; morning was here and the sun was bright. I looked down at myself in amazement. I hadn't had a bath in days and my clothes smelled of sweat and vomit. I felt distant and numb. I walked with Michael down the hall and into the lounge where we usually held our morning therapy sessions. I didn't feel like talking and I don't think I heard anything that he might have said. It all seemed so ineffectual. I felt as if I had just been paroled from the "Big House." I knew that the only information that Michael had regarding the events from the night before was just what had been charted by the night nurse. I didn't have the will or the desire to explain. Nothing mattered. I don't even think that at that particular time I even possessed the strength to try and explain — the desire just wasn't there. I was simply a terrible, neurotic woman, with maladaptive responses to both my stresses and this hospitalization. "C'est la vie."

chapter nine

One of the things which I really tried to deal with while I was hospitalized was some of the issues regarding my mother. It had been clear to me for the past two years what my father's role had been in my abusive childhood, but I could never truly understand that of Mama's. Michael said that I should keep a journal and write some of the flashbacks down, so that we could explore them during some of our upcoming sessions, but I just couldn't.

I remember her last days. The days when she was dying and lay in the hospital withering away. It was in 1983; I was married and had two small babies and the whole ordeal was very taxing for me emotionally. I couldn't believe that she was actually dying. As I lay in my bed at Divine Angels Hospital, thinking about her death, I was overwhelmed. So many things were going on in my life. I was looking forward to my discharge, and Michael wanted me to start to deal with my mother! It wasn't until I was discharged and safe in my own home with my husband and children that I felt strong enough even to think about her.

To the rest of my family she had been some kind of self-sacrificing "Goddess," but after all that I had been through, and after all of the information that had been revealed to me, she was just as responsible for some of the abuse as my father was. When she died, however, none of this information was available to me and I was just as vulnerable as the rest of my sisters and my brother. To this day, there are no pictures of Mama in my house. I don't really know why, but my life, Mama, and the pain of my childhood are just a little bit more than I can stomach. The question of her whereabouts while I was being tossed about throughout the "system" and living on the streets is a reality which I find extremely hard for me to try and focus on. It's hard to write about her and when I try, I find myself "doubling-up" on the antidepressants and becoming submerged in both her pain and mine. My lack of understanding regarding her treatment of me and her coldness aches me to the core. I mean, it's right up there with "Doom, despair, agony, deep-dark depression, and excessive misery!!!!" (Excuse me, while I vent.)

Shortly after my discharge from the hospital, in December, I became very ill. I was bleeding and decided to get to my gynecologist as soon as possible. It was discovered that the enlarged uterus, which was found on the IVP test taken while I was in the hospital, was actually a giant fibroid tumor.

My gynecologist, Dr. Wright, hauled me away to yet another hospital, called Pine Valley, for emergency surgery. I was told that the tumor was benign but because it was pushing down on my bladder and uterus that I had to undergo a complete hysterectomy. At twenty-nine years of age, I felt that my body was failing me; it had deceived me into believing that I could after all of my sexual abuse, have a "normal" life, as a "normal woman" — Ha!! Still, I went through with this surgery. After all, what options did I have? There had been second opinions and they all led to this big drastic step.

The pain and suffering afterwards was unbelievable! It was just a few days before Christmas, and I had already spent both Halloween and Thanksgiving Day in the previous hospital, so I was now determined to make sure that I was not going to spend Christmas in this one. I had the surgery done quickly and asked to be released two days later.

"Mrs. Birts, the usual time for recovery for this type of surgery is at least four days," the attending doctor said to me.

"I know, but I don't have four days to spare. My children need me home sick or not, and that's where I want to be." So, with his approval I was discharged. It was hard wanting to do more than I was really able to do, but at least I was home. My sister, Ann, came by and helped me to decorate the house for the children's Christmas and I sat in the corner of the dining room depressed and aching, while I tried to put up a good front for everybody else.

I could never really stop the flashbacks and tried desperately not to think about the horrible Christmases of the past, when I was growing up. But like everything else in my life, I had little or no control of such surging memories or reoccurrences. The hardest flashback that I tried to fight off was that of my father pulling out his gun one Christmas and demanding that we, his children, get our "asses" out of bed on Christmas Eve and get our own presents out of the trunk of his car. I was very young and still believed in the myth of good old "Santa Claus," so this was a big dose of reality being thrown like a brick into my face, not to mention the hard lesson I learned at that tender age. There my father stood, as drunk as he wanted to be, holding a gun to my sister Jerry's head demanding that we carry our own presents from the car and place them under the tree. "I'm Santa Claus," he mused, half staggering and falling over onto the Christmas tree. "If you want to know who bought these presents, I bought them. . . ."

"What a life," I thought, as I brought my mind back to 1990 and the beautiful tree that was standing in my front living room. My children knew the true meaning of Christmas and I would never put them through such terror. But that was just the point. "What mother in her right mind would allow her babies to be subject to such humiliation and abuse?" This is a question that I'll probably go to my grave asking and wondering about. "Mama, Why? How?"

"Mama why didn't you help me, why, Mama? I know times were hard for you too, but for whatever reasons, you couldn't, or didn't help your children. But I got through most of it regardless, didn't I, Mama?" Yep, I got through it, and I'm still "getting through it." My New Year's resolution for that year was to be a good wife to my husband,

and the best mother for my children, and to beat my depression!

I wanted to continue with my therapy and get on with my life. I had recently joined a support group for survivors of incest and was doing a little counseling with battered women. Reaching out and listening to the pain of others seemed to help me in taking the focus off of my own pain. It didn't do away with it, but I felt that I wanted to be there for other women in my similar situation. Even with the work that I would do with these abused women and children, I had to sit back and have my own little anxiety attacks from time to time. I knew that the odds were against me, but I felt as if I were slowly finding my way back home. I had a good therapist, a good psychiatrist, support from my family doctor, Dr. Roberts, but most of all, I felt that I wanted to make it.

Two months after going through with my hysterectomy, I once again began to feel this penetrating pain in my pelvis. "There isn't much left of me," I thought, as I sat in the gynecologist's office. "I only have half an ovary left. . . ." I thought I would die while being examined by my doctor. "What the heck is that?" I screamed out as he was examining me.

Without an answer he slipped his hand into my rectum and began a more thorough probe. All throughout this examination I was having one of my anxiety attacks. I had known this doctor for all of my life — he brought me into this world, he delivered both my children, and when anything was wrong, he was always frank and open with me. Slowly, he took off his rubber gloves and told me to get dressed and that he would be right back. After what seemed like hours he entered the room and stated that he had made arrangements for me to undergo an ultrasound because of what he felt during my exam and because of the pain that I was experiencing. He explained that what he felt was a very large and infected ovary. "Depending upon the findings of this ultrasound, I feel that I have to be honest and tell you that if it looks as big and infected as it feels, we'll have to remove it."

I was stunned. It was all that I had left. It was the only female organ that hadn't been tampered with, but most of all, medically speaking, it was the only thing that I had left after my hysterectomy that was making intimacy with my husband bearable. After the hysterectomy, I had begun to experience vaginal atrophy, penetration was painful, and now I was being told I might be losing that little bit.

I walked slowly down the street. I couldn't cry; I didn't want to cry. I was tired and stopped at a local restaurant to get a glass of water to wash down my pain pill.

Dr. Wright was correct in his findings. The ultrasound uncovered an ovary four times its normal size, replete with disease and an ovarian cyst attached at the lower base of the ovary, equally as large. I hated my life and I hated everything about living. "I need time," I told Dr. Wright, after the results. "I just need time." He was explicit in laying out to me what the repercussions of my procrastinating might lead to, but he never pushed me for another surgery. He knew that I was tired. Michael, on the other hand, stated that I was playing "Russian Roulette" with my life by not entering into the hospital immediately, but I just needed time. I was scared. I was tired and somehow I had to take this all in.

It didn't seem to be a hard decision for other people to judge, but for me, well, that was a different story. I felt like a Jew straight out of the Old Testament of the Bible, when they would "rent" their clothing as a sign of utter pain and agony.

"Just get it over with. Have the surgery. It's better than taking a chance and allowing that cyst to burst, because then, not only will you still be dealing with that diseased ovary, but you'll be dealing with all that fluid and its potential of forming tiny little cysts throughout all of your pelvis." These were the sentiments of most of the people around me; it was an easy call for them.

Menopause at age 29!! Boy, how do I continue to be so lucky? Why, I was just thinking yesterday . . . **"Hey, I have this one, tiny, insignificant ovary left over from my hysterectomy. It's not doing much good; why don't I save myself some trouble and just have the little ungrateful organ ripped from my body right now? Better yet, let's do it as soon as possible — this week for example. The sooner the better!! Then, and only then, will I be able to appreciate what every other 'real' woman from forty-seven to sixty years of age is experiencing. Yep, menopause, that's what I've been missing in my life . . ."** (Sorry, but I had to digress there just for a moment!!)

I listened — but I didn't hear. It just wasn't fair. It just wasn't fair! Hadn't I been through enough? Wasn't I trying to pull my life back together? Wasn't I? I walked around for about a week filled with hatred. It was directed toward anything and everybody who entered into my sick little circuit. I was on a silent rampage. I fought with myself, although I knew the stronger side would win, and it did.

Fred and I attended a lecture for menopausal women (one of which I would soon become).

The speaker was very thorough in answering any questions which either of us had. I guess being on "Estrogen Replacement Therapy" for the rest of one's life isn't the end of the world. When we walked into the room, I couldn't help but notice that it was filled with women ages fifty and older (or so it seemed). Most of these women had already reached menopause, and wanted more information regarding their new lives and what they could expect during this change of life. Of course, I was asked by someone standing at the door if I knew what group I was attending. I stared directly into her eyes and said, "Yes, unfortunately. . . ."

This book doesn't have a wonderful, happy ending because I don't feel wonderful or happy. I feel tired and drained. Incest and life will do that to you. I continue to have flashbacks surrounding those horrible days as a child, I still wake up in cold sweats over nightmares regarding my father molesting me, but there is always my husband, Fred, lying beside me, holding me, soothing me and telling me that "It's all right to cry, it's all right to feel the pain, but after you feel it, you have to let it go." And that's what I'm learning. I'm learning to feel the pain, to cry and then to let it go. It's not as easy to do as it sounds, but it is possible. While I was at the hospital, during my last stay I ran across a little poem that I have to include in this book. It's by an unknown author and it goes like this . . .

"I am worth celebrating. I am worth everything, I am unique, in the whole world there is only one me. There is only one person with my talents, experience, and gifts. No one may take my place.

God created only one me, precious in his sight, I have immense potential to love, care, create, grow, sacrifice — if I believe in myself.

It doesn't matter my age, or color, or whether my parents loved me or not. (Maybe they wanted to but were unable.)

It doesn't matter what I have been, the things I've done, mistakes I've made, people I've hurt. I am forgiven. I am accepted, I am okay. I am loved in spite of everything.

So I love myself and nourish seeds within me. I celebrate me. I begin now, start anew. I give myself a new birth today. I am me, and that's all I need to be.

This is a new beginning. A new life given freely, so I celebrate the miracles and I celebrate me."

— Author unknown

Incest is a terrible, terrible thing for any child to have to go through and live with for the rest of his or her life. It is a physical violation of a child's body through any sort of sexual contact, or a psychological violation of the child through verbal or nonverbal, inappropriate sexual behavior. It is neglectful, disrespectful and harmful because it violates a child's basic right to be protected, nurtured, and guided throughout his or her childhood. Whether it was covert actions of abuse or overt actions, it is all sexual abuse and as parents we have to take heed of the warning signs.

In my quest for both knowledge and an understanding of sexual abuse, I was stunned at some of the myths yet circulating regarding incest and the abusers. The most common myth that I ran across was that childhood sexual abuse is usually committed by a stranger — a pervert, a child-attacker on the streets — but, in fact the vast majority of childhood sexual abuse is perpetrated by family members, and the majority of the offenders are fathers and step-fathers. It was for this reason that I felt led to give this feeble account of some of my struggles as both a child and an adult, trying to put the shattered pieces of my life back together. For all of my life I have felt that I was this "dirty" or "nasty" little girl. Prior to therapy, I didn't know where this all stemmed from, but over the years, I have been able to get at the true root of the problem — incest.

When I remembered myself in a flashback, actually going to my father for him to abuse me, I shuddered at that memory and felt that I really wanted it, or was asking for it. In fact, all I ever wanted from this man was what most little girls want from their fathers and that was to be loved and held (in a non-sexual way) and to be told that he loved me. The isolation that I felt after the first assault on my young body did away with any "normal" relationship between my father and myself.

In many ways I feel that I have been re-traumatized by the Medical Community in itself, but I also feel that along with my struggles, "going it alone" has made me a stronger person. It has put me in the place to help other incest survivors like myself. Incest survivors don't need to be put through the meat grinder. We need to be reassured on a constant basis that "It wasn't your fault. You were an innocent child, and this abuse was perpetrated against you." But there don't seem to be that many people out there with that message.

This book is meant to hug and hold every woman that is going through the recovery process from incest "victim" to that of incest "survivor," because that's just what it is — a process. It doesn't happen overnight and there are no "magic pills" to make the pain go away (if there were, I wouldn't be in the shape that I'm in).

I want to hold every survivor in my arms — all of you and tell you that it is okay to cry. Cry all you want, and when you are finished, cry some more. Confront your abuser if you feel that you must, but have a good support system to fall back on, and I will always be with you in spirit. Talk about your feelings with a good supportive friend or a good therapist. This will assist you in learning compassion for the little lost child who survived and endured all the hurts, pains, and fears which you feel now as you remember and relive your past. Allow yourself to cry for the child who you were. Picture yourself as that child and reach for her. I find that when I hurt the most, it's not the adult in me that's hurting; it's my inner child and sometimes they are inseparable.

I hated the little pitiful Briéanna and have been pretty rough on her at times. No one wants to be faced with this wide-eyed, abused, needy person all of the time. So I, like many of you, have tossed her aside in my mind — just as I was tossed aside. When I came to a point that I felt that I really wanted to be totally whole, it was then that I fell to my knees and literally reached for her. I had to tell myself that little Brié was a real part of me and sometimes she wanted and needed some of the little things that she never received as a child.

For example, I find myself from time to time watching cartoons, blowing bubbles on a clear day — it soothes the aching child within me, and I must tell you, those simple things that I just listed were very difficult to do. Society as a whole has "standards," and "guidelines" regarding what an adult is, and how an adult should conduct his or herself, but I have found that when I'm alone in a loving and safe environment some of little Brié's needs can be met. I talked recently to a friend who told me that she had always loved the zoo and longed to visit it, however she had no children of her own to stroll around the grounds with. Subsequently, she started baby-sitting other people's children just to satisfy her own child-like fantasies. This demonstrates a perfect example of the daily hurt and frustration that people have to go through in order to get some of their basic needs met. I myself am no different than she. I bought into all of the negative things that my father hurled at me. But time has taught me that "Briéanna, you are not a whore, you are not a slut. You are a good and lovable person (who will probably be in therapy for the rest of your life)."

I haven't reached that proverbial "Mountain Top." I wrestle with deep depression, which I am told I will live with for the rest of my life, but I have finally found the strength to reach way down from within the depths of my soul for that little lost Briéanna, who hid in her closet with "Patches" and "Sallyanne," and have found the will to love and take care of her and to slowly tear down some of her secret hiding places.

I don't know where Mama was, or why she couldn't or didn't help me — but it doesn't matter anymore because where Mama was weak, I have been empowered to be strong.

Wanna' hear a joke? (It's a blast!!) I talked to Dr. Bly yesterday, and he says that they have this new drug that he thinks will really help me!! It's an MAO Inhibitor. . . . "It'll take only about a ten-day stay in the hospital. . . ."

"Yeah, right, Doc, hold that thought. . . ."

RECOMMENDED READING

Angelou, Maya. *I Know Why the Caged Bird Sings.* New York: Bantam, 1980.

Armstrong, I. *Kiss Daddy Goodnight.* New York: Hawthorn, 1978.

Brady, Katherine. *Father's Days: A True Story of Incest.* New York: Dell, 1979.

Bronson, Catherine. *Growing Through the Pain.* Park Ridge, Illinois: Parkside Publishing, 1989.

Butler, Sandra. *Conspiracy of Silence: The Trauma of Incest.* San Francisco: Volcano Press, 1985.

Forward, Susan, and Craig Buck. *Betrayal of Innocence: Incest and its Devastation.* Los Angeles: Jeremy P. Tarcher, 1978.

Gil, Eliana. *Outgrowing the Pain.* New York, New York: Dell Publishing Co., 1983.

Herman, Judith. *Father-Daughter Incest.* Cambridge: Harvard University Press, 1981.

Morris, Michell. *If I Should Die Before I Wake.* New York: Dell, 1982.

Rush, Florence. *The Best-Kept Secret: Sexual Abuse of Children.* Englewood Cliffs, N.J.: Prentice-Hall, 1980.

NATIONAL RESOURCES

To find the resources available in your area please call or write to the following National Organizations:

Parents Anonymous
22330 Hawthorne Blvd., Suite 208
Torrance, CA 90505
(800) 352-0386

Parents United/Sons and Daughters United
   (sexual abuse treatment)
P.O. Box 952
San Jose, CA 95108
(408) 280-5055

National Center of Child Abuse and Neglect (NCCAN)
Dept. of Health and Human Services
P.O. Box 1182
Washington, D.C. 20013
(202) 245-2856

C. Henry Kemp National Center for the Prevention and Treatment of Child Abuse and Neglect
1205 Oneida St.
Denver, CO 80220
(303) 321-3963

LOCAL RESOURCES

Child/Adolescent Center
St. Mary's Hill Hospital
2350 N. Lake Dr.
Milwaukee, WI 53211
(414) 271-5555

The Counseling Center
2038 N. Bartlett
Milwaukee, WI 53211
(414) 271-4610

Hillside Office-New Concepts:
636 W. Kneeland
Milwaukee, WI (414) 271-7496
Self Development Center/Sexual Assault Program for Black Youth

Milwaukee Council on Alcoholism
2266 N. Prospect Ave., Room 324
Milwaukee, WI 53202
(414) 276-8487
24 hours

Parents Anonymous Family Sexual Abuse Program
1717 S. 12th St.
Milwaukee, WI 53204
(414) 671-5575

Rape-Sexual Assault Treatment Center
Good Samaritan Medical Center
2000 W. Kilbourn St.
Milwaukee, WI 53233
(414) 937-5555

Sexual Assault Treatment Center
Sinai Samaritan Medical Center
2000 W. Kilbourn
Milwaukee, WI 53233
(414) 937-5555

Task Force on Battered Women
4067 N. 92nd St.
Wauwatosa, WI 53222
(414) 466-1660

Wagner Clinic
700 W. Michigan St., Suite 405
Milwaukee, WI 53233
(414) 272-8485

The Women's Crisis Line
(414) 937-5463 *24 hour crisis line*

HEARING IMPAIRED SERVICES

Office for the Hearing Impaired
819 N. 6th St., 6th Floor
Milwaukee, WI 53203
(414) 963-6567

Milwaukee Hearing Society
TTY Crisis Line
(414) 271-6039
Counseling, Therapy Available

HISPANIC SERVICES

Council for the Spanish Speaking, Inc.
614 W. National Ave.
Milwaukee, WI 53204
(414) 384-3700

International Institute of Wisconsin
1110 N. Old World Third St., Suite 420
Milwaukee, WI 53203
(414) 225-6220